The CIA

During the Second [World War ...] [spe]nt
three years [...]
with the co[...]
Ninth Air [...]
keen intere[st ...]
has written [...]
subject. His [...]
volumes.

He is the fo[rmer] editor-in-chief of two
encyclopedias for young people – *Compton's* and
The American Educator. Don Lawson now devotes
all of his working time to writing books for
children.

Also in the
Spy Shelf Series
by Don Lawson

The French Resistance
The KGB

 **Piccolo Spy Shelf**

The CIA

Don Lawson

A Piccolo Original

Piccolo Books

First published 1986 by Pan Books Ltd,
Cavaye Place, London SW10 9PG
9 8 7 6 5 4 3 2 1
© Don Lawson 1986
ISBN 0 330 29212 9
Photoset by Parker Typesetting Service, Leicester
Printed and bound in Great Britain by
Collins, Glasgow

This book is sold subject to the condition that it
shall not, by way of trade or otherwise, be lent, re-sold,
hired out or otherwise circulated without the publisher's prior
consent in any form of binding or cover other than that in which
it is published and without a similar condition including this
condition being imposed on the subsequent purchaser.

Contents

1 'Caught in the act'	7
2 Forerunners of the CIA	14
3 How the CIA is organized	36
4 Spies in the sky	49
5 The CIA and the Bay of Pigs	57
6 Dark and bloody deeds	67
7 The CIA invades the 'Halls of Ivy'	78
8 The CIA in the Vietnam War	86
9 The 'family jewels'	97
10 The Soviet spy who came in from the cold	109
Appendix: directors of the Central Intelligence Agency	119
Bibliography	120
Index	122

1
'Caught in the act'

In the autumn of 1984 it became known that a recently published United States Central Intelligence Agency (CIA) booklet contained do-it-yourself directions on political assassinations and the overthrow of a foreign government.

The existence of the eighty-nine page booklet and its CIA sponsorship were revealed by the Associated Press. Entitled *Psychological Operations in Guerrilla Warfare*, the publication was intended for use by Nicaraguan guerrillas or *contras* who were trying to overthrow their country's so-called Sandinista government.

While the guerrilla handbook used the word 'neutralize' in speaking of how 'selective violence' could be most effective in eliminating various public officials, there was little doubt that neutralize meant assassination. The guerrilla guide went on to suggest that 'professional criminals be hired' to provoke the shooting of certain people – 'court judges, police, and state security officials'.

News of the existence of such a manual, which smacked of the very terrorist tactics that the United States government had long condemned, caused a public outcry. Congressman Edward Boland, Chairman of the House Intelligence Committee, said the booklet was 'repugnant to a nation that condemns such acts by others. It embraces the communist revolutionary methods that the United States is pledged to defeat throughout the world'.

Since the disclosure occurred right in the middle of a national election campaign, Democratic partisans sought to condemn the Republican Administration for the booklet's publication. The Democratic Party's candidate for president, Walter Mondale, immediately attacked his opponent, incumbent President Ronald Reagan, by saying, 'Did he know this was going on? I don't know which is worse – knowing this was going on or having a government where no one is in charge.' Mondale also demanded the immediate resignation of CIA Director William Casey.

President Reagan, via a White House spokesman, responded by disavowing any connection with the guerrilla handbook. The press was also reminded that the booklet violated an Executive Order signed by President Reagan in 1981 prohibiting even indirect participation in assassinations. (Two previous presidents, Gerald Ford and Jimmy Carter, had also issued such Executive Orders.) It was also announced that President Reagan had ordered an immediate investigation. 'This Administration has not advocated or condoned political assassination or any other attacks on civilians, nor will we,' said White House spokesman Larry Speakes.

Unfortunately, this was not the first time the CIA had been openly accused of being involved in assassination attempts and other illegal actions against foreign leaders and their governments. Some of these alleged abuses went back as far as the 1950s, just a few years after the CIA was born. They included the overthrow of the Jacobo Arbenz government in

Guatemala; an attempt to overthrow the government of Chile and prevent Salvador Allende from becoming that country's duly elected president; attempts to assassinate Cuba's Fidel Castro, Congolese leader Patrice Lumumba, Rafael Trujillo of the Dominican Republic, and Chilean General René Schneider; the capture and murder of Ché Guevara, Latin American revolutionary; and finally, the participation in the coup against South Vietnam's President Ngo Dinh Diem, which resulted in his death.

Because of their extremely serious nature these alleged abuses were investigated by the United States Congress. In 1975 the Church Committee, so called because it was headed by Senator Frank Church, issued a report entitled *Alleged Assassination Plots Involving Foreign Leaders*. The report's conclusion was that the CIA was not directly responsible for the deaths of any foreign leaders. Questions about the indirect involvement of the CIA went largely unanswered, and the Church Committee's head himself was quoted as saying that the CIA 'might have been rampaging out of control like a rogue elephant'.

To say the least, the American public and media were more than a little sceptical about the innocence of the CIA in all of the alleged abuses. Where there was smoke, was the general belief, there must be some fire. As an indication of this scepticism, people began to say that the initials CIA should stand, not for Central Intelligence Agency but, instead, for 'Caught In the Act'.

In an attempt to repair the CIA's image, as well as to prevent future abuses, permanent CIA Oversight Committees were established in both the House of Representatives and the Senate. In addition, the Agency's original charter was revised by the presidential

Executive Orders formally making illegal any and all attempts direct or indirect to assassinate foreign leaders.

These moves proved effective until the 1980s when the CIA became, actively and more or less openly, involved in the overthrow of the Nicaraguan government. Congressional leaders, including those on the Oversight Committees, were taken by surprise in 1983 when it became known that the CIA had directed the placing of explosive mines in Nicaraguan harbours. Under most circumstances such activity is regarded as an act of war. Subsequently, this act was condemned by the International Court of Justice in the Hague, but the Reagan Administration defended itself by insisting that it was combating the spread of communism in Central America, including its export from leftist Nicaragua to neighbouring El Salvador and Honduras.

CIA Death Squad connections?

In the spring of 1984 even more serious charges were once again levelled against the CIA. This was the suggestion that the Agency had some connection with army and intelligence units in El Salvador that had engaged in the torture and killing of Salvadorian citizens. These 'Death Squads' had long been a subject of severe criticism by the American media and most members of the US Congress.

On 8 May the *Christian Science Monitor* ran an article that alleged that these Death Squads had been operating with the knowledge of the CIA and other US government officials. At about the same time Senator Edward Kennedy raised the question of whether or not the CIA was indeed involved in supporting Death

Squad activities. Kennedy cited a story that had appeared in the *New York Times* alleging that a Colonel Nicolas Carranza, former chief of the terroristic Salvadorian Treasury Police, had received more than $90,000 a year from the CIA as an informant for the past several years. Carranza, it was alleged, had engaged in Death Squad activities.

These allegations resulted in an immediate investigation by the Senate Oversight Committee. Several months later the Committee issued a report stating that all allegations that the CIA or any other US Government agency or officials had any connections with Salvadorian Death Squads were false.

A few feeble cries of 'Whitewash!' went up around the nation when the report was issued, but by this time most Americans had forgotten what the investigation was about. But the *Monitor*, Senator Kennedy, and the *New York Times* all continued to express doubts about the truth of the Oversight Committee's findings.

Meanwhile, stories about the publication by the CIA of the guerrilla assassination handbook began to make headlines, and the possible CIA Death Squad connection was all but forgotten.

Rogue elephant again on the loose?

The first person actually to defend the guerrilla guide was the head of the CIA, William Casey. On 24 October 1984, Casey sent a two-page letter to the members of the Congressional Oversight Committees in which he claimed the actual purpose of the manual was 'educational'.

In his letter Casey insisted that the manual's 'thrust and purpose' were 'on the whole, quite different from the impression that has been created in the media'. Casey went on to say that the manual's actual purpose was 'to make every guerrilla persuasive in face-to-face communication'. Casey's letter added that the manual's 'emphasis is on education, avoiding combat if necessary'.

The Casey defence was not greeted with open hoots of disbelief but with a major measure of scepticism by most members of the Oversight Committees. The manual did, after all, explicitly advocate 'the selective use of violence' to overthrow the Nicaraguan government – a clear violation of the CIA charter.

Had the CIA once again become a 'rogue elephant', this time rampaging out of control in Central America? This was the question that the American public and the media began to ask. The answer would not be forthcoming for many weeks or perhaps even months when the Congressional Oversight Committees completed their investigations and issued their reports.

But even though President Reagan had said that any CIA official involved in development or approval of the guerrilla manual would be dismissed, few observers expected any such serious action would be taken. By the time the Oversight reports became available most of the public and the media would have lost interest in the matter, and it would probably be passed over as a mere 'tempest in an intelligence teacup'. President Reagan himself indicated the line the Administration would take when, even before the reports were in, he said that the translation of the guide was faulty. Instead of 'neutralizing' Nicaraguan leaders, he said, the translation should have read 'remove'.

'If that technique is followed,' said one Congressional leader, 'the guerrilla guide will wind up sounding like a poor translation of the Boy Scout Handbook.'

But there were those who thought the publication of the CIA guerrilla guide raised a more serious question – a question that had arisen each time the CIA was once again caught in some flagrant act. That question was, is there a place in a free society like the United States for an intelligence agency that by its very nature must engage in secret or covert activity, activity that may very well ignore human rights and human freedoms? In other words, does or can the United States Central Intelligence Agency play a legitimate role in an open, democratic society by destroying some of the very rights it is charged with defending?

To answer this question we must go back to the reasons for the founding of the CIA and examine the history of its activities.

2
Forerunners of the CIA

Until relatively recently the United States did not have a peacetime civilian secret intelligence organization. Before World War II most Americans frowned on such activities. Perhaps Secretary of State Henry L. Stimson expressed the general feeling best in 1929 when he said, 'Gentlemen do not read other people's mail.'

Needless to say, the American public in general and Stimson in particular changed their minds when the Japanese attacked Pearl Harbor, Hawaii, on 7 December 1941. Stimson had become Secretary of War by this time, and he was well aware that faulty coordination and interpretation of US peacetime military and naval intelligence had made such a surprise attack possible. In addition, the American people, rudely awakened from their peacetime slumbers, began to demand an organization that would provide better secret intelligence information in the future.

Meanwhile, however, there was a war to fight, and to do so successfully an immediate espionage operation was a must. Wartime spy services were not new to the United States. In fact the nation had had one in every war since the American Revolution. During World War II this spy organization was called the Office of

Strategic Services (OSS). Headed by Major General William 'Wild Bill' Donovan, a hero of World War I, the OSS played a key role in Allied espionage activities on the European continent during World War II (see *The French Resistance*).

After the Allied victory over Germany, Italy, and Japan in World War II, US President Harry S. Truman decided that a peacetime espionage organization was needed. By this time a so-called 'Cold War' had developed between the Soviet Union and the Western nations, and President Truman persuaded Congress that such an intelligence organization was vital for the protection of American interests that were being threatened by the Soviet Union. Thus, in 1947, the Central Intelligence Agency (CIA) was born.

The early CIA had few guideposts to follow. Most foreign countries, of course, had their own intelligence organizations, but these were patterned after the special nature of the nations they served. The CIA had to establish an intelligence operation that met the special needs of the United States. Consequently, CIA planners looked to the history of America and American espionage. Since the nation had never before had a peacetime spy service, lessons had to be learned from the records of earlier wartime spy organizations kept by their leaders. The first of these leaders was no less a person than the nation's first president.

America's first spymaster

George Washington was not only the first president of the United States. Even before he became president he was also the nation's first spymaster. The first American intelligence service, which was organized by

Washington, was called the Culper Ring. The Culper Ring was a network of American Revolutionary War spies who operated against the British enemy along the East Coast, mainly in the New York area.

Washington decided to organize an efficient intelligence service following the capture and execution by the British of one of America's most famous spies – Nathan Hale. A handsome young schoolteacher and former athletic hero at Yale University, Hale joined the American patriots' army in 1775 as a first lieutenant. Soon promoted to captain, he fought under General Washington in what was at first a losing cause.

While fighting in and around New York City, Washington needed to know the number of British troops opposing the Revolutionary Army and where they were located. (This is called the 'order of battle' and has always been a prime target of agents.) Young Captain Hale volunteered to get this information. Dressed in civilian clothes, he crossed through the British lines on Long Island and carried out his spy mission. But while trying to return to the American lines he was captured by the British. The maps and notes concealed in his pockets disclosed Hale's mission, and he was ordered to be executed as a spy by General William Howe.

Hale was hanged on the morning of 22 September 1776. As he stood on the scaffold the young patriot uttered his now-famous words: 'I regret that I have but one life to lose for my country.'

Following Nathan Hale's death, General Washington named another of his officers, Colonel Benjamin Tallmadge, to organize and train a group of men in the business of espionage. Tallmadge had been a friend and classmate of Hale's at Yale, so he set about the task eagerly. He saw it as a way to avenge his friend's death. Washington himself worked closely with Tallmadge and his spy trainees, offering sound, basic advice.

Once they had crossed through the British lines and entered New York, Washington told them to 'mix as much as possible among the officers and refugees. Visit the coffee houses and all public places.' Washington also told them to keep their eyes and ears open. By doing so they could probably gain vital information about 'defence works being thrown up on Harlem River near Harlem Town, and whether Horn's Hook is fortified. If so, how many men are kept at each place and what number and what size cannon are in those works.' Washington's need for information was remarkably similar to that of any modern military commander.

Washington's spy service was called the Culper Ring because one of its best agents or spies, Abraham Woodhull, used 'Samuel Culper Senior' as a code name. In addition, one of Woodhull's best sources of information in New York, Robert Townsend, had the code name 'Samuel Culper Junior'. Townsend was a quiet young Quaker merchant whom the British regarded as a man of peace who wanted no part of the war on either side. But Townsend was a staunch patriot as well as a Quaker and was ready to die for the American cause.

Like all good spy networks before and since, the way the Culper Ring worked was relatively simple – and highly dangerous. Information was gathered in New York, which was the British military headquarters, by numerous private citizens who pretended they were sympathetic to the British cause. Most of these Americans were merchants and tradespeople who had frequent business contacts with British officers. In addition to Townsend, one of the best of these information gatherers was a tailor named Hercules Mulligan.

Mulligan was generally avoided by his pro-rebel American neighbours, mainly because he was so friendly with the enemy and seemed to be pro-British. Actually, the tailor was busy getting valuable intelligence information from his talkative red-coated customers. All of this information he passed along to General Washington via the Culper network.

Abraham Woodhull (Culper Senior) was the first link in this network. Woodhull operated out of a local boarding house where Townsend, Mulligan and other local agents delivered their espionage reports. From this raw data Woodhull prepared single-page reports. These were picked up by a local farmer named Austin Roe who appeared in New York regularly to deliver his produce and buy his own supplies. On horseback, Roe in turn delivered Woodhull's reports to a boatman, Caleb Brewster, who crossed Long Island Sound by night and delivered them to Colonel Tallmadge. Tallmadge, in turn, handed the reports over to General Washington whose headquarters were along the Hudson River.

At Washington's headquarters another now-famous early American, Alexander Hamilton, was most often the person in charge of coding and decoding spy reports and developing the messages that were written in invisible ink.

Woodhull's greatest fears were of being betrayed by the capture of any of the Culper Ring's messengers by the British. The messages they carried would, of course, have been a complete give-away. This danger was overcome by the use of a simple code suggested by Washington and developed by Tallmadge. The code substituted numbers for the names most commonly used in the messages. Washington, for example, was 711, New York was 727, Long Island 728, etc. Numbers were also assigned to all prominent British officers as well as the members of the Culper Ring itself. This meant that both Woodhull and Hamilton had to have copies of the key to the code, and its capture would have been disastrous.

Although some of its sources of information *were* occasionally caught, the Culper Ring itself was never compromised. None of the merchant-agents who were caught ever gave any information about the spy ring even though they were promised their freedom if they talked. A dozen or more went silently to their deaths when they could have saved themselves by talking. Woodhull himself lived in constant fear of his life because the boarding house where he lived was mainly occupied by British officers. But their presence actually helped make his spy nest an ideal 'safe house'.

To eliminate virtually all risk invisible ink was finally used by Woodhull and Hamilton. This remarkable fluid, called Sympathetic Stain, was developed in London by Sir James Jay, brother of American patriot John Jay. Sir James favoured the American cause and passed along his Sympathetic Stain to his brother John. This ink became invisible as soon as it was applied to white paper and only became visible again when another secret chemical liquid was brushed over it. The formula for both of these liquids has never been discovered, although other invisible inks have since been developed.

Using the Sympathetic Stain, the sender could simply write a spy report or a request for intelligence information between the lines of an innocent-looking letter. The receiver could then brush the paper with the required substance and the invisible ink became instantly visible. Sympathetic Stain was, however, in short supply and since Sir James would not tell how it was made the Culper Ring had frequently to struggle along without it.

Spy costs worth the money

Just as is the case today, espionage efforts were expensive during the American Revolution. Washington kept careful records of what he and the Culper Ring spent in buying information. Washington paid this money out of his own pocket and then later billed the Continental Congress for his expenditures. Frequently he spent more than he ever got back. As Allen Dulles, former Director of the CIA, has stated in his book *The Craft of Intelligence*, Washington 'spent around $17,000 on secret intelligence during the years of the Revolutionary War, a lot of money in those days'. Today this sum would amount to approximately $750,000.

But there is little doubt that this money was well spent. In fact America might well have lost its War of Independence without the work of the Culper Ring, which also performed valuable counter-intelligence work. It was, for example, mainly responsible for the discovery of the most famous traitor in American history, Benedict Arnold.

Arnold, one of the most successful of the Revolutionary Army's officers, became bitter over not receiving a promotion in rank or credit for several successful campaigns which he led. Because of what he regarded as his country's ingratitude, Arnold decided to turn over West Point to the British when he was placed in command of the military fortress on the Hudson in 1780. In planning this treachery Arnold corresponded with a British officer, Major John André, in New York.

The Culper Ring entered the picture when talk of the plot reached Robert Townsend in New York. Townsend immediately forwarded the information to Washington's headquarters where plans were put in motion to arrest Arnold. Before he could be arrested, however, Major André was caught while trying to make his way through the American lines on a pass issued to him by Arnold.

André's arrest alerted Arnold, and he fled to the British in New York. Although Arnold escaped and later served with the British Army, historians agree that if his planned treachery had not been discovered it would have resulted in a serious if not fatal blow to Washington's forces. Control of the Hudson, where West Point was a key bastion, was of vital importance to Washington and his Continental Army.

Until the modern era, few American wartime espionage efforts have been so successful as Washington's during the Revolution. A major advantage that the Culper Ring had, of course, was the fact that both the rebels and the Redcoats spoke a common language. Thus American agents could frequently gather information simply by eavesdropping on conversations among the enemy.

In several later wars a lack of knowledge of the enemy's language was a severe handicap to American agents. This necessitated the recruiting of spies among the enemy population, not always an easy – or safe – thing to do. Great care had to be taken, for example, to make sure the recruited spy was not a double agent – that is, someone who was actually loyal to the enemy while pretending to be loyal to the United States. Double agents are a problem that continue to plague the CIA as well as all other intelligence agencies to this very day.

During the Mexican War of 1846 and the Spanish American War of 1898, the United States Army had notable success in recruiting agents among the enemy populations. Army intelligence in the Mexican War was headed by Colonel Ethan Allen Hitchcock, whose given name was that of a hero of the Revolution. Colonel Hitchcock organized a company of spies from among the Mexican civilian population and deserters from the Mexican Army. This company along with a network of spies in Mexico City itself was the best American intelligence system since Washington's day.

Although the United States conquered Cuba in a few months in the Spanish American War, guerrilla warfare against the American forces in the Philippines dragged on for several years. The insurrectionists waging this guerrilla warfare were led by a Filipino nationalist patriot named Emilio Aguinaldo. As long as Aguinaldo remained free the guerrilla warfare threatened to continue indefinitely.

Finally, early in 1901, American General Frederick Funston turned a group of Aguinaldo's Spanish-speaking rivals into double agents who led the Americans through enemy territory to Aguinaldo's secret headquarters. There the insurrectionist leader was captured and the fighting in the Philippines ended.

Fighting against the American Indians presented almost impossible espionage problems during the War of 1812 and the later Indian Wars in the West and Southwest. Not only were the Indian nations closed societies into which it was all but impossible for a white agent to infiltrate, but Indian battle plans were also frequently spontaneous, spur-of-the-moment affairs so an agent could give no forewarning of them.

The American frontier army did, however, utilize information gained from scouts, trappers, and traders who travelled among the Indian tribes and could at least report on their numbers and locations. Occasional renegade redmen could also be bribed to give valuable information. But it was not until the Civil War, when a common language was spoken by members of both the northern and southern armies, that espionage again became a valuable weapon.

Lincoln the spymaster

Abraham Lincoln proved to be every bit as expert a spymaster as George Washington. And yet it was an espionage failure that finally allowed the great Civil War president to be assassinated.

A private detective, Allen Pinkerton, headed Lincoln's spy ring early in the war. When Lincoln was on his way from Illinois to Washington to be inaugurated in 1861, there were numerous rumours that he would be killed even before he took office. When Pinkerton got Lincoln to Washington without incident – mainly by arranging to have the inaugural train move through major Eastern cities secretly by night – the private detective and his operatives earned the job of permanently protecting the president.

But once the Civil War began, Pinkerton proved to be a better bodyguard than a collector of intelligence. When Lincoln realized this, he proceeded on his own to hire a man named William A. Lloyd 'to proceed South and ascertain the number of troops stationed at different points in the insurrectionary States, procure plans of forts and fortifications, and report the facts to the president'.

For his efforts Lloyd was to be paid his expenses and $200 a month. He successfully carried out his mission all during the war, constantly avoiding capture by the Confederates. But he was not so successful in getting paid for his efforts, never receiving much more than his expenses.

To put espionage on a more organized basis, later in the war Lincoln established the Bureau of Military Information. General George H. Sharpe was put in charge of this Intelligence Bureau, which met with varying degrees of success. Feeding Sharpe and his Bureau valuable intelligence were two Northern loyalist volunteers, Elizabeth van Lew and Lafayette Baker.

First American woman spy

Elizabeth van Lew was loyal to the North although she lived in Richmond, Virginia, capital of the Confederacy all through the Civil War. Here she accomplished that most difficult of all wartime feats, the penetration of the home of the enemy head of government. She did this through one of her black servants who worked as a maid in the home of Jefferson Davis, president of the Confederacy. The maid, who helped serve meals, was able to report all conversations among the military men who dined at Davis' table, and these conversations were in turn passed on by her mistress, Elizabeth van Lew, to General Sharpe in Washington.

The van Lew coup was called by both Lincoln and General Ulysses S. Grant the most valuable spy effort of the war. There was no doubt about Elizabeth van Lew's loyalty to the Union during the Civil War, nor was there any doubt about her fellow spy Lafayette Baker, who also supplied the North with valuable information.

Baker the photographer spy

Baker was a photographer who toured Confederate camps taking pictures of the rebel soldiers to send home to their families. During his travels Baker picked up valuable order of battle information which he managed to forward to General Sharpe in code along with his orders for additional photographic supplies from a Washington supply house.

Baker was so successful that he was eventually placed in charge of the National Detective Police to replace Pinkerton who had gradually faded out of the picture as the presidential protector. Baker's original police organization has since become the US Secret Service.

However, there has always been something of a mystery about Baker. The mystery surrounds Lincoln's assassination on 14 April 1865. The question has long been asked: where were Baker and his National Dectective Police on the night of the assassination? Lincoln's box at Ford's theatre on that tragic evening was mysteriously unguarded and the whereabouts of the guard that normally should have been there is still unknown.

First peacetime military and naval organizations

It was not until some years after the Civil War, in the 1880s in fact, when the first peacetime military and naval intelligence organizations were formed by the United States. These, of course, were staffed by military and naval personnel, not civilians as is the CIA. In addition, little or no effort was made to coordinate the intelligence-gathering efforts of the two organizations. In fact, inter-service rivalry virtually prevented such cooperation, a situation which was eventually to result in the surprise attack on Pearl Harbor.

The Army intelligence organization was known as the Military Information Division. The Navy organization was called the Office of Intelligence. By the early 1900s Army intelligence became the second division among several other types of divisions under the Army General Staff and thus became generally known as 'G-2'. It is still called this today. During World War II the US Army Air Corps (later Air Forces) created its own intelligence division which was called 'A-2'. The Navy organization grew into the Office of Naval Intelligence or simply ONI.

Neither Army nor Navy intelligence was at first regarded by service regulars as an organization that would lead to the advancement of their military or naval careers. In fact an assignment to intelligence was long thought to be a dead-end job. Consequently, by the time the United States entered World War I in 1917 the country once again was without any real intelligence service.

World War I espionage

At the start of World War I the United States gained order of battle information and all other necessary intelligence about the German enemy from the French and British. This was not in the least satisfactory since America was generally regarded as a johnny-come-lately into the war by its two major allies and received only the intelligence that France and Britain felt like parting with. Soon an American wartime intelligence organization was again established, and before the war ended in 1918 had accomplished some notable espionage feats.

The US World War I military intelligence organization was at first headed by Colonel Ralph H. Van Deman. Van Deman was succeeded by General Dennis E. Nolan and General Marlborough Churchill. Working closely with these three espionage experts was future CIA Director Allen Dulles, who was also to play a key role with the OSS in World War II. In both world wars Dulles operated out of Switzerland, a neutral country where he could not be captured by the German enemy.

Probably the most important single intelligence development to come out of World War I as far as the United States was concerned was the great improvement of America's codes and ciphers. This improvement was accomplished almost single-handedly by Herbert Osborne Yardley. Yardley also made great strides in deciphering other countries' codes and ciphers.

Yardley and America's 'Black Chamber'

In Yardley's day both the making and breaking of codes were lumped together and called *cryptography*. Today this term is used simply for the making of codes. The breaking of codes is called *cryptanalysis*. Together the two kinds of code work are called *cryptology*.

When World War I began, cryptography (today's cryptology) was in its infancy. Fortunately, the United States had Herbert Yardley on its side at this key stage in the making and breaking of codes. From an early age young Yardley had proved to be something of a genius at all kinds of code work.

Code making and breaking had been a hobby of Yardley's from the time he was a teenager in his home town of Worthington, Indiana. His father had been a railway telegrapher. While watching and listening to his father operate the telegraph at the local train depot young Yardley had quickly learned the meaning of the dots and dashes of the Morse code. From there he had gone on to create his own codes and ciphers which his father was unable to break.

(The words *codes* and *ciphers* are often used to mean the same thing. Actually, codes usually involve the use of whole words, while ciphers usually involve the use of single letters. Codes and ciphers are created by shifting the normal letters in a word from one place to another – *transposition* – or exchanging a word for other letters, words, symbols, or numbers – *substitution*.)

In his early twenties Yardley decided to go to Washington where the only work for his particular talent seemed to be available. In the nation's capital he got a job as a $900-a-year code clerk and telegrapher in the

US State Department. Here his supervisor was surprised – and not a little disturbed – to learn that Yardley was quickly and easily able to read the encoded and supposedly secret cables that crossed his desk on their way to and from foreign embassies.

While the State Department was debating what to do about Yardley and his obvious talent, World War I began and he quickly joined the Army as a second lieutenant. Fortunately, Lieutenant Yardley's military superiors knew what to do with him and despite his low rank he was placed in charge of all code and cipher work for Military Intelligence.

Since *he* was soon able to break and read most intercepted German military and diplomatic messages, Yardley assumed that the Germans were also able to read American 'secret' communications. As a result, Yardley quickly established a Code Compilation Section within Military Intelligence that created new and much more difficult code systems. He also established a Code and Cipher Solution Section that by war's end was breaking and reading all foreign encoded messages as easily as if they had been sent in the clear or uncoded. During the course of the war, Yardley's organization deciphered almost eleven thousand messages sent by foreign governments.

When World War I ended in November of 1918, it appeared that once again the United States would simply abandon its intelligence-gathering efforts as the nation returned to peacetime isolationism. But both the Army and the State Department saw enormous possibilities in being able to eavesdrop on foreign communications even in peacetime. This could be done not only by intercepting cable messages but also messages sent by radio, which was fast becoming an international communications medium.

In a secret agreement signed in the spring of 1919 the US State Department and US Army agreed to the establishment of a peacetime code and cipher organization similar to that run by the Army during World War I. The only difference was that this so-called 'Black Chamber' would be manned by civilians with Yardley in charge. The Black Chamber, however, would be funded by both the Army and State Department from secret funds. The fact that the Black Chamber was to be manned by civilians and its budget was to be secret made it the closest operation to today's CIA that had been established up to this point. But the Black Chamber was not intended as an international intelligence-gathering organization with human spies active in the field. It was purely and simply aimed at intercepting and decoding all foreign communications traffic via cable and radio.

The work of the Black Chamber was almost immediately dramatically successful. At its secret headquarters in New York City the Black Chamber was fed foreign cable traffic by carefully screened communications experts in Washington. Within a matter of months Yardley and one of his assistants, Frederick Livesey, were able to crack the Japanese secret diplomatic code.

But this early triumph proved to be the Black Chamber's high point. Soon the peace and booming economic prosperity of the Roaring Twenties had set in across the land and few people, including officials in Washington, seemed to be much interested in foreign affairs. The Black Chamber's supply of intercepted cables and radio messages gradually began to dry up. Then, in the late 1920s, Congress passed legislation that made it illegal for anyone to receive radio or cable communications unless such messages were addressed directly to him or her. This effectively ended the Black Chamber's secret operation.

Yardley did not give up, however. When Herbert Hoover became president in 1929 and selected Henry L. Stimson as his Secretary of State, Yardley approached Stimson about the possibility of the State Department's continuing to secretly supply Yardley with all intercepted messages from foreign powers. Up to this point Stimson did not know that the Black Chamber existed. He was outraged when he learned about it and told Yardley that the Black Chamber was a strictly illegal operation. Stimson then went on to make his classic comment about gentlemen not reading other people's mail.

Partly in anger and frustration and partly because he needed the money – by the 1930s the United States was in the midst of its worst economic depression and jobs were few and far between – Yardley began to write a series of magazine articles and a book about the Black Chamber. Yardley's revelations created a national and international sensation rivalling the later uproar over CIA excesses. Some efforts were made by the War Department to prevent the publication of this material but to no avail, and Yardley's book was a bestseller for many months. Today it lies all but forgotten on many dusty library shelves.

Meanwhile, both US Army Military Intelligence and the Office of Naval Information continued the cryptological work begun by Yardley. In the Army this was handled by the Signal Corps and in the Navy by the Office of Naval Communications. Both organizations specialized in intercepting and decoding radio messages, especially those being sent and received by the Japanese.

Before the start of World War II these organizations

had broken both the Japanese Navy codes and the new Japanese 'Purple' or diplomatic codes. But no success had been gained in breaking the Japanese Army code system. This was finally achieved in 1943 in the middle of World War II with the aid of the British at their Wireless Experimental Centre in India.

Although both the Japanese Navy and diplomatic codes had been broken prior to the surprise attack on Pearl Harbor, there was little or no effort made to coordinate the Japanese communications traffic that was being intercepted and decoded. No central signal office received, read, and evaluated this traffic and passed on the information to key people. It simply came pouring into Washington or to various command posts in the Pacific theatre of war and key people might never see it. The president got some of it, the State Department got some, some went to Army and Navy chiefs of staff, and much simply lay about unevaluated in top-secret file baskets where it was not seen until weeks or even months after it could have been useful. Thus the adequate warnings about Pearl Harbor mainly went unnoticed or at least not generally understood and acted upon until it was too late.

Postwar security measures

It was to prevent such a situation arising in the future that not only the CIA but also the National Security Agency (NSA) were established soon after World War II. Although the CIA was established first, in 1947, it did not take over the modern Black Chamber, highly technological work of intercepting and decoding international communications. This became the job of the NSA.

President Harry S. Truman signed a presidential Executive Order creating the National Security Agency on 24 October 1952. The move was so secret that for a long time few people knew such an order had been signed, and it was years before it was generally known that the NSA existed. Today Yardley's primitive Black Chamber efforts have come to full flower in the super-secret and super-sophisticated NSA which intercepts and monitors much of the world's communications traffic. No longer do today's NSA Black Chamber efforts depend merely upon being fed cable traffic or upon intercepting radio and cable messages. It utilizes its own satellite eavesdropping system and computerized recording devices at listening posts throughout the world.

Although it is many times larger than the CIA and spends many billions of dollars more per year, the NSA is still not known about by many Americans. And yet this super-secret agency provides some of the most valuable kinds of intelligence of any espionage organization in the world. Its technological listening posts and its spies in the sky filter back to Washington the most minutely detailed bits of communications – from a Soviet general in Moscow talking on his car telephone to communications among Russian fleet commanders during naval war games in the Atlantic.

But signals intelligence (SIGINT), which is what the NSA's product is called, can only capture and record worldwide communications. It cannot know what prompted such messages, interpret their meaning, or predict probable future enemy activities. This is still the work of human intelligence (HUMINT), which is where the CIA still plays a vastly important role.

Birth of the CIA

When the OSS began operation during World War II its main function was as a research and analysis organization. Under the guidance of the flamboyant Wild Bill Donovan, however, it soon grew into a full-blown espionage organization with agents aiding the various anti-German underground networks in Europe and North Africa. Although the OSS also operated in the China-Burma-India (CBI) theatre, it did little work in the Pacific theatre of war where Commander Douglas MacArthur did not welcome its presence. MacArthur had set up his own espionage and intelligence system and did not want it tampered with by anyone outside his own command.

In Europe the OSS had outstanding success working closely with the French Resistance, the British Special Operations Executive (SOE), and various partisan groups in Central Europe. Sabotage and other resistance activities helped make possible the defeat of both Germany and Italy. Near the end of the war the OSS was also instrumental in hunting down and capturing numerous enemy war criminals and collaborators.

But when World War II ended, all of this active foreign espionage effort was abruptly brought to a halt. Soon all that remained of the OSS was its intelligence-gathering staff in Europe and its research and analysis branch in Washington. These too were threatened with elimination.

But almost immediately after the war the Soviet Union, which had fought with the Allies against the Axis powers – Germany, Italy, and Japan – began to take over several formerly free countries in Eastern Europe. These included Poland, Rumania, Bulgaria,

Hungary, Albania and Czechoslovakia. The Western nations, principally the United States, France, and Great Britain, opposed this totalitarian takeover by the Soviets and soon a so-called Cold War set in between Russia and the free nations of the West.

Many Western government leaders believed that the Soviet Union was bent on spreading its oppressive communist form of government not only throughout Eastern Europe but also throughout the world. One of those who believed so was US President Harry S. Truman. In order to prevent the spread of communism as well as to prevent the pre-World War II type of intelligence failures, President Truman believed the United States badly needed an intelligence organization that would keep the American government informed about whatever secret plans the Soviet Union had for any future totalitarian aggression – not only in Europe but also in Asia.

With this in mind Truman asked OSS Chief Donovan to draw up plans for a permanent central intelligence agency. Donovan did so, and in 1947 Congress passed the National Security Act which incorporated much of the Donovan blueprint. Thus the United States Central Intelligence Agency was launched. At first the CIA was to have smooth sailing in calm seas. But within a very few years it was to encounter extremely stormy weather and the heavy seas of violent public criticism would threaten to founder it.

3
How the CIA is organized

President Harry Truman always claimed that he never had any idea that when he set up the CIA that it would become involved in peacetime 'cloak and dagger' spy work throughout the world. Nevertheless, almost immediately that is exactly what happened, and CIA international espionage activity has continued ever since. In fact much of the CIA is organized for just that purpose.

Overall, the CIA is headed by a director and deputy director. Under them are actually two organizations divided into numerous subsections. The first of the two major divisions is called the Deputy Directorate of Information (DDI) which probably fills the passive CIA role Truman had in mind. It is a central place for bringing together all of the raw intelligence available to the government. Here the raw intelligence is analysed for its meaning and importance and summary reports are written and provided for key members of the government. The president, for example, has a top secret intelligence summary from the CIA waiting for him on his desk when he arrives in the Oval Office each morning. Annually, the DDI also prepares an intelligence estimate of the world military, political, and economic situation and a survey of Soviet intentions and capabilities.

Workers in the various subdivisions of the DDI are research specialists. Many are multilingual scholars. They may be, for example, engineers who are fluent in the Russian language. These men and women carefully read all engineering papers, magazines, books etc. published in the Soviet Union and its satellite nations. From their reading these specialists may detect discoveries of scientific trends inside communist countries. This information is painstakingly recorded and any valuable nuggets of intelligence are extracted and put into reports. Other specialists in other areas of knowledge – political scientists, economists, historians, physicists, electronics theorists etc. – pursue a similar research routine. Their research is not, of course, restricted to Soviet publications, but its emphasis is on them. In addition, intelligence from the second major CIA division is fed to the DDI to be assessed and analysed.

The second division of the CIA, and the one that has always received the most media attention, is called the Deputy Directorate of Operations or DDO. The DDO is the clandestine or secret organization which is actively involved in international espionage. Within the Agency itself the DDO is usually called Clandestine Services.

The importance of samizdat

Another valuable source of information about the Soviet Union is underground literature, which is called *samizdat*. This is pamphlets, books, or exposé material of any kind secretly written by dissidents within the Soviet Union who oppose the Soviet regime. Some of this material is actually printed by the underground inside Russia, but much is smuggled out, printed, and then smuggled back into the country where it is sold on the black market.

The CIA plays an active role in obtaining *samizdat*, assessing its contents, and then 'reinserting' it into the Soviet Union. Soviet sailors have long been a valuable source as couriers for carrying *samizdat*. The reason for reinserting underground literature into Russia and making it available on the black market is because it is thus given much more widespread distribution than it would get otherwise.

Among the best-known books that have been smuggled into the Soviet Union has been Boris Pasternak's *Doctor Zhivago*. More important is a publication called the *Chronicle of Current Events* which lists all dissident activity as well as various arrests and trials. Both are black market bestsellers.

Number of employees and annual budget

Shortly after it was founded the CIA had some 5,000 employees, only a handful of whom (mostly former OSS operatives) were serving overseas. Today it is the world's second largest intelligence organization (the Soviet KGB is by far the largest). The CIA has between 16,000 and 18,000 employees, some 5,000 of whom officially serve abroad. Actually the number of its workers in foreign countries is much larger. Literally tens of thousands of mercenary soldiers, consultants, agents and other temporary or long-term employees are hired by regular CIA personnel to perform certain jobs. The actual number of these 'contract employees' is difficult to determine because it varies from year to year and assignment to assignment. One such contract employee in Nicaragua was reportedly responsible for preparing the guerrilla guide told about in Chapter 1.

Recruiting foreign agents is one of the main jobs of CIA station chiefs or case officers assigned to duty outside the United States. A station chief's or case officer's success, in fact, is generally determined by the number and quality of agents he hires and the value of the intelligence they produce. While station chiefs or case officers do not have unlimited budgets, they nevertheless can usually get whatever amount of money they need to pay foreign agents and purchase the intelligence they seek. Some of these funds are accountable, but far from all.

Overseas the CIA also actually controls certain legitimate businesses which it uses as cover for some of its agents. These are called 'proprietary companies', and they include everything from small manufacturing businesses to several small airlines. Interestingly, some of these proprietary companies are run so well that they actually make a profit and do not have to be subsidized by the CIA.

The CIA's authorized annual budget runs to about $1 billion (one thousand million in US terms). Here again the figure is actually much larger, but much of the money it spends is hidden in a secret contingency fund controlled by the director of the Agency who is accountable only to the president. In addition, money is secretly fed to the CIA by the Pentagon. Pentagon sources supply the CIA with hundreds of millions of dollars a year, depending upon immediate CIA needs. Former CIA station chief John Stockwell has stated that a certain covert action in Africa 'cost American taxpayers a million dollars a day for a sustained period'. It has never been made known – and probably never will be – how much money the CIA spent during the Vietnam War. A similar situation existed regarding CIA activity in Central America during the 1980s, although Congressional oversight committees made valiant if futile efforts to obtain specific spending statements from CIA Director William J. Casey. But Stockwell has also stated that: 'The Congress has neither the will nor the means to control the CIA.'

CIA headquarters and 'the Farm'

Headquarters for the CIA is in Langley, Virginia. Located on a wooded 125-acre site, the headquarters building was first opened in 1961. It is surrounded by a high, barbed-wire-topped fence patrolled by armed guards and guard dogs. Before 1961 CIA offices were scattered all over nearby Washington, D.C., and some are still located there. A processing centre for new employees is located in Arlington, Virginia, and numerous other small offices are located elsewhere in Virginia. Employees who must travel among the various sites are served by hourly shuttle buses and limousines.

Like most other office buildings the CIA headquarters is only open for business during the day. At the end of each work day all desks must be cleared and secret material placed in safes or put through a shredder or into burn bags to be incinerated. At night security forces patrol the building and any papers found unsecured are collected and the persons guilty of leaving papers on their desks are reported. A sufficient number of demerits for security violations can lead to dismissal. The CIA hesitates about firing personnel because a disgruntled former employee may be inclined to disclose secret information, but the Agency is nonetheless rigid in its security measures.

All of the headquarters janitorial staff, including cleaning women, must undergo security clearances. In addition to the security forces – one of whom follows each cleaning lady about – a duty officer and his small staff remain on duty each night to receive incoming cables or any other urgent messages. The duty officer immediately reports any emergency situation to his superior. At 3.00 A.M. a special staff arrives to prepare the president's daily intelligence summary, which is a digest of various intelligence information sent by station chiefs throughout the world. The CIA has a remarkably efficient worldwide computerized cable network. Via an emergency cable, called FLASH or CRITIC, a station chief anywhere in the world can report a crisis to Langley in no more than seven minutes. Such cables are in the process of being coded, transmitted, received, and decoded while they are being composed.

The training of new CIA case officers for work with the clandestine services takes place at another location. This is a 480-acre establishment outside Williamsburg, Virginia, that is known as 'the Farm'. Actually it bears the name Camp Peary and looks like a normal military post with barracks, offices, classrooms, and recreational facilities. Also on the grounds are weapons firing ranges, parachute jump towers, and – hidden in the woods away from public view – a Hollywood-like set that closely resembles a real-life communist community with sealed-off borders.

Recruitment

In the beginning the CIA recruited heavily among the so-called 'Ivy League' schools, Harvard, Yale, Princeton, etc. This was because the CIA's roots were in the OSS, and the OSS was always oriented toward the 'Eastern Establishment' and the Ivy League colleges and universities. Outsiders, in fact, often joked about the initials OSS standing for 'Oh So Social'. The exclusive Ivy League network to which most early CIA members informally belonged was identical to the Old Boy network to which many Oxford and Cambridge university graduates in British Intelligence circles belonged, beginning in the 1930s. (See *The KGB*.)

But during the Vietnam War the CIA became discredited for its clandestine activities in Laos and Cambodia as well as for the coup against South Vietnam's President Diem. Since then Ivy Leaguers have avoided the CIA, and Agency recruiters have had to look elsewhere for prospective trainees. This has meant recruitment on college campuses throughout the country as well as in the armed forces.

The CIA carries on its recruitment program much like any other large business. Ads are run in newspapers. Recruiters visit college campuses where professors recommend students as possible candidates. Candidates are also suggested by CIA personnel, and outstanding ex-military intelligence officers are frequently hired. The CIA, however, is far from being an equal-opporunity employer and is frequently accused of being undemocratic in its selection process. Other than in clerical positions the Agency has only a comparatively small percentage of blacks among its employees. In addition, few women have attained top roles anywhere in the Agency except perhaps in the research area. Women clandestine agents are virtually non-existent, but a few are hired abroad.

All prospective CIA employees must take lie-detector tests. Their backgrounds and personal history are also thoroughly investigated. Once they are hired any new employees – including women secretaries – destined for overseas service are given a short course in espionage tradecraft. This may include surveillance techniques and the recruitment of agents. Specialized spy training, however, is reserved for what the Agency calls 'career trainees' or CTs.

Just what qualities does the CIA look for in a prospective CT? Former Director Dulles has said such prospects must 'be perceptive about people, be able to work well with others under difficult conditions, learn to discern between fact and fiction, be able to distinguish between essentials and non-essentials, possess inquisitiveness, have a large amount of ingenuity, pay appropriate attention to detail, be able to express ideas clearly, briefly and, very important, interestingly, and finally, learn when to keep your mouth shut'.

Ex-Director Dulles went on to add that 'a good intelligence officer must have an understanding for other points of view, other ways of thinking and behaving, even if they are quite foreign to his own. Rigidity and closed-mindedness are qualities that do not spell a good future in intelligence'.

Dulles also pointed out that 'an intelligence officer must not be over-ambitious or anxious for personal reward in the form of fame or fortune. These he is not likely to get in intelligence work. But he must bring to the task that intangible quality which is one of the most necessary of characteristics of an intelligence officer – motivation.'

Motivation, Dulles concluded, 'comes from an

awareness of the conflict that exists in the world today, a conviction that the United States is involved in this conflict, that the peace and well-being of the world are endangered, and that it is worth trying to do something about these things.'*

This same kind of motivation might well lead an intelligent, idealistic, patriotic young man into the State Department or Peace Corps or religious missionary activity. But intelligence work has an added element of raw adventure that has a powerful appeal to most potential CIA case officers. Almost daily they can see evidence of the enemy in action and as case officers they are the cutting edge of their country's efforts to combat that activity.

Training

Once career trainees or CTs are hired they are put through a rigorous two-year training program during which they are on probation. One year of this training is in the US and the second year is spent abroad.

Much early training is devoted to instilling in the trainees a feeling of dedication to the CIA and its goals. On the white marble walls of the foyer at Langley headquarters is the inscription: 'Ye shall know the truth and the truth shall make you free.' It is in this spirit that training classes are conducted. CTs learn the history of the CIA and its organization as well as how it differs from other nations' intelligence agencies. They are also taught the importance of security and the two types of intelligence activity, research and surveillance or espionage. Security and secrecy must

*Dulles, Allen, *The Craft of Intelligence*, Harper and Row, New York 1963.

become a way of life to all CIA personnel not only while on the job but also in their personal relations, including those with their families. As prospective clandestine operatives they are taught how to collect intelligence by covert or secret means and actual covert action, or the intrusion into the affairs of foreign countries by secret means. An important course is also given on the nature of international communism and trainees soon learn that the Soviet Union is the 'enemy'. This type of indoctrination is similar to that taught to US military trainees, although the CIA course is in greater depth. Past triumphs of both the CIA and Soviet KGB are dramatically illustrated in specially produced training films. Films, in fact, play a major role in all training classes. Numerous Hollywood-produced spy movies are shown and trainees are asked to criticize the agents' techniques in their film spy roles.

Down on the Farm

At the Farm CTs are given what amounts to basic infantry training followed by more advanced military training. This includes learning to fire all kinds of hand weapons, how to use explosives for demolition work, and how to load and fire light artillery. Some of these more advanced skills are not taught because the trainee will eventually use them himself but so that he will be able to teach them to hired paramilitary personnel.

Every trainee destined for the clandestine services must also make a certain number of actual parachute jumps after training on the parachute towers. Advanced training in explosives and demolition and the use of heavy weapons is given at North Carolina's Fort Bragg and, until recently, at Fort Gulick in the Panama Canal Zone where jungle combat training was conducted during the Vietnam War.

All during the course of their CIA schooling CTs study the making and breaking of codes and ciphers. They also have the opportunity of attending foreign language classes – this is encouraged – and all are required to infiltrate the mock-up of the communist 'country' within the Farm's confines. Once inside this country trainees are rated on their ability to avoid capture. Once captured they are further rated on how well they stand up under enemy interrogation. Trainees adopt false names and invent cover stories to disguise their true indentities during this part of training. Students try to learn anything they can about other students, including their real identities, and are given merit points for breaking their colleagues' cover.

At Fort Bragg top CIA candidates are given the opportunity to undergo the rigours of the 'survival course' designed for Green Beret candidates. The Green Berets are members of America's elite special forces military organization who are widely regarded as the nation's most self-sufficient soldiers. The survival course designed for them requires candidates to live off the land in an enemy-occupied wilderness environment. This means eating native vegetation and wild life – including snakes – while avoiding capture for a period of days and sometimes weeks. No CT is given demerits for flunking this course, although Green Berets *must* pass it.

Once a CT's first year of schooling is over, he is given on-the-job training for another year at an overseas post. This usually means being assigned to a

United States embassy under cover as a State Department foreign officer. The trainee may also be sent abroad as a businessman working for one of the CIA proprietary companies or for some normal business concern with offices abroad, and some are attached to military installations. But most CIA officers in foreign countries work under State Department cover. This same practice is followed by most foreign intelligence services.

In his foreign post the CT learns at first hand how to recruit agents and gather intelligence by working directly with a veteran CIA officer. If he passes this course, the CT is returned to Langley for assignment to a regular foreign post as a full-time station chief or case officer. He is now virtually independent, but he is also charged with the full responsibility for all covert action in his area.

It is interesting to note that while foreign governments may not be aware of the identities of another country's intelligence officers in their midst, KGB agents always know and recognize their CIA or British counterparts. (The American and British intelligence services work closely together.) Likewise, CIA officers know who the local KGB agents are, and British intelligence agents are equally well informed. But contrary to the James Bond stories and other modern spy fiction, American and Soviet or British and Soviet agents do not waste their valuable time running about trying to kill one another. What they seek is intelligence information and to this end gangster-type warfare among agents would be wholly unproductive. Interservice intelligence rivalry does frequently become intense. The spreading of false information or so-called 'disinformation' is a frequent method of counter-intelligence attack in this ongoing conflict. Getting an enemy agent to defect is another and perhaps most effective counterstroke. But almost never are there duels to the death among agents.

4
Spies in the sky

One of the most successful of all the CIA's Clandestine Services officers was Richard Bissell. He also became one of its greatest scapegoats.

Bissell joined the CIA in 1954. By 1958 he had become the head of Clandestine Services. In 1961 he was forced to resign from the Agency by President John F. Kennedy. During his few brief years in the CIA, however, Bissell completely revolutionized the Agency's methods for gathering intelligence about the Soviet Union. And even after he was fired Bissell was retained as a civilian consultant because his services were too valuable for the CIA to do without.

Bissell was a brilliant economy student at Yale University from where he graduated in 1932. Later he earned his Ph.D. in economics and taught the subject at both Yale and the Massachusetts Institute of Technology. During World War II he worked in Washington, and after the war he was one of the economists who developed the Marshall Plan to rebuild and feed Western Europe. It was from this post that he was recruited to join the CIA.

One of Bissell's first assignments was to try and figure out how to carry on disruptive covert action within the Soviet Union and its Eastern satellite

49

countries. His conclusion was that under then-current conditions carrying on any kind of disruptive covert acitivity within the Soviet police state was next to impossible. Bissell's frustration over being forced to this conclusion later led him to the achievement of his greatest intelligence feat.

Meanwhile, however, Bissell was called upon to take part in the overthrow of a communist government in Latin America. US government officials had viewed with increasing alarm the postwar spread of communism in Eastern Europe and were determined to keep it out of the Western hemisphere. Their immediate target was Guatemala where communist sympathizer Jacobo Arbenz was in power.

Not only had Arbenz legalized the Communist Party in Guatemala and invited it to become a part of his government, but he had also forcibly seized half a million acres of banana plantations owned by the American United Fruit Company. At one time such events would have meant military action, but now President Dwight D. Eisenhower and his Secretary of State John Foster Dulles decided to turn the matter over to the CIA, where the Secretary of State's brother, Allen Dulles, was then director. By this time Bissell was Allen Dulles' special assistant for Planning and Coordination, so Bissell was given a key role in planning the Guatemala operation for which $20 million had been earmarked by the Eisenhower Administration.

The Guatemala coup against Arbenz worked brilliantly. Colonel Carlos Castillo-Armas, a Guatemalan army officer who had been trained at the US Army Command and Staff School at Fort Leavenworth, Kansas, was selected to lead the anti-Arbenz forces. While Castillo-Armas trained a rebel force of several hundred men in Honduras, a CIA-sponsored radio propaganda campaign was launched throughout Latin America in the spring of 1954. Secretary of State Dulles also cooperated by publicly denouncing the Arbenz regime.

In June Castillo-Armas and his 'army of liberation' crossed over into Guatemala and advanced to within a few miles of the capital, Guatemala City. The actual size of the small band of liberators was disguised by continuous CIA broadcasts of lengthy military orders and reports of fictitious major battles so that the Arbenz defenders thought a major military force was advancing against them. At the same time Castillo-Armas's 'air force' of three US P-47 fighter planes put up a show of force by flying low over the capital and harmlessly buzzing the frightened populace. In addition, CIA contract pilots flying US Air Force planes that had been 'sold' to Nicaragua by Richard Bissell flew over Guatemala City and dropped two or three small bombs. At the end of June Arbenz resigned and Castillo-Armas entered the capital and took over the government.

In government circles this bloodless CIA coup was hailed as a resounding success. A communist threat to the Americas had been eliminated without official US intervention. But most Latin Americans were fully aware that the CIA had been responsible for the coup and were insulted by the action. Resentment of the CIA was to grow throughout Central and South America in the months and years ahead.

But Richard Bissell was far too busy with what he and a handful of his Agency colleagues regarded as a much more important project to take time out for praise or blame for the Guatemala operation. Spurred on by a stubborn determination to gain access to the inner secrets of the Soviet Union, Bissell was now concentrating all of his considerable intellectual powers in working to perfect a reconnaisance or spy plane that could fly directly over the Soviet Union at such a great height that it could not be shot down. While it was still on the drawing board this remarkable plane was known as the 'Black Lady'. Later when one such plane *was* shot down and it became world famous, or perhaps more aptly infamous, it was known as the U-2.

The U-2 had first been the idea of the US Air Force. Bissell became involved with the project when President Eisenhower decided that the revolutionary spy plane should be developed in secrecy and turned it over to the CIA. The CIA agreed to pay some $22 million to the Lockheed Aircraft Corporation for building the plane. Actually it cost several million dollars less than the original estimate.

Bissell and Lockheed also went to heroic lengths to develop the Black Lady in much less time than the six years that the Air Force had estimated it would take to produce an operational model. Bissell and the half a dozen members of his project development staff officially began work in mid-1954, and the first U-2 underwent a test flight just a year later. Bissell and his men worked seven days a week during that year, maintaining such secrecy that not even Director Dulles knew the details of the project.

Once the plan was ready for testing Bissell selected a training site in Nevada at the Atomic Energy Commission's proving grounds. This assured continued secrecy. Originally Strategic Air Command (SAC) pilots were assigned to fly the plane, but they in turn taught civilian pilots the extremely difficult job. Once the plane became fully operational the government did not want to risk having one downed by the Soviets with an American Air Force officer aboard. Nevertheless, once the plane proved to be successful the Air Force tried to regain control of its operation. This was disapproved by Eisenhower and the CIA retained its control of how, when, and where the spy plane was to be used.

In all, by the spring of 1956 some twenty-two U-2s were built, and an operational wing was stationed in Turkey. The wing consisted of four U-2s and six civilian pilots plus a ground staff of several hundred men. In June the first U-2 took off on its first mission to fly over the Soviet Union from Turkey to Norway.

'The flight was a complete success,' author Thomas Powers has said. 'The Russians immediately picked up the U-2 by radar – Bissell had hoped the U-2 might even be too high for radar, but that hope was in vain – but they were unable to do anything about it. At 80,000 feet, its cameras photographing a swathe on the ground 120 miles wide, the U-2 sailed soundlessly across the Soviet Union far beyond the range of Russian anti-aircraft missiles, and it continued to fly at irregular intervals for nearly four years.'*

Interestingly, while the Soviets were immediately aware of the U-2 reconnaisance flights over their territory, they seemed to be as determined to keep them a secret as were the Americans. Probably this was because they did not want their own people to know that they were vulnerable to this spy in the sky until they had developed a similar observation plane themselves.

But the Russians did continue to try and shoot down the U-2s, and finally, in May of 1960, they were successful. The U-2 was brought down by a ground-to-air

*Powers, Thomas, *The Man Who Kept the Secrets*, Alfred A. Knopf, New York 1979.

anti-aircraft missile called a SAM which badly damaged the plane and forced its pilot, Francis Gary Powers, to bail out. After the plane crashed enough of it was left undamaged for the Russians to put it and the uninjured Powers on public display in Moscow for all the world to see what war mongers the Americans were.

Unfortunately, Powers and his U-2 were brought down on the very eve of a scheduled summit conference between President Eisenhower and Soviet Premier Nikita Krushchev. The incident forced the conference to be cancelled, and the Soviets continued to make international headlines for weeks afterwards by exploiting the effectiveness of their own defensive devices. No mention, of course, was made of how effective the plane had been for several years.

Just how effective the plane *had* been was also summed up by author Powers, who has said: 'Bissell's (U-2) programme brought in more hard intelligence than all previous sources put together ... It made it impossible for the Soviets to lay a sewer pipe in Siberia without the CIA learning about it.'

Although all U-2 flights over the Soviet Union were cancelled following the Powers incident, the plane continued to be used with great effectiveness over communist China by pilots flying out of Taiwan, and over communist Cuba by pilots flying out of the United States.

After long negotiations Powers was released by the Russians in exchange for an American-held Soviet spy, Colonel Rudolph Abel, in 1962. After his return to the United States Powers flew a news helicopter for a TV station in Los Angeles. He was killed when his helicopter crashed in 1977.

Bissell's success as head of the U-2 project led to his

being made deputy director of plans, or head of Clandestine Services. But more importantly the U-2 was merely the forerunner to today's ultra-sophisticated satellite spies-in-the-sky.

The immediate successor to the U-2, however, was not a satellite surveillance platform but another super-secret winged plane called the 'Blackbird', or SR-71. Bissell also helped develop this phenomenal reconnaissance aircraft which flew at heights of up to 90,000 feet at speeds of almost three and a half times the speed of sound. The Blackbird could attain such speeds because it had a skin of heat-proof titanium. It was also able to photograph 100,000 square miles of the earth's surface in less than an hour. In addition, it had sensors that could detect electronic installations on the earth's surface and side-looking radar that could penetrate well into the Soviet Union while flying along one of its borders. No Blackbird was ever shot down, but it was soon replaced by the all-seeing reconnaissance earth satellites.

The use of orbiting satellites for espionage platforms became feasible in 1960. That summer a US C-119 jet transport plane flying near Hawaii at a height of about 10,000 feet was able to retrieve in a huge net which it trailed a capsule ejected moments before from the Discoverer 14 satellite orbiting the earth overhead. This capsule contained photographs taken automatically by Discoverer while flying over Soviet territory. The capsule was immediately flown to Hawaii where the crystal-clear photos were developed. Almost immediately the United States and the Soviet Union began an espionage satellite space race which continues to this day.

The US satellite intelligence system is a direct outgrowth of Bissell's development of the U-2 and the

SR-71. It was regarded as so important by government officials, however, that as soon as it became practical its operation was turned over to a special organization known as the National Reconnaissance Office (NRO). The NRO is actually run jointly by the CIA and the Air Force, but it is a so-called 'black' agency whose very existence is denied by the US government.

Unfortunately, Richard Bissell was not destined to become a key member of the highly classified NRO. In fact the year the agency was formed, 1961, was the same year both Russell and his mentor, Allen Dulles, were asked to resign from the CIA. Their downfall occurred because of the CIA-planned invasion of Cuba at the appropriately named *Cochinas* Bay, or Bay of Pigs.

5
The CIA and the Bay of Pigs

Soon after he came to power in Cuba in 1959 Fidel Castro became a thorn in the side of the United States. Castro and his followers, called 'Fidelistas', had overthrown the oppressive dictatorship of Fulencia Batista, and it was at first widely believed that the Castro regime would be much more democratic than Batista's. Almost immediately, however, the Castro dictatorship proved to be as harsh and oppressive as Batista's. In addition, Castro proclaimed his government would be communist.

Like Arbenz in Guatemala, one of the first things Castro did was seize property in Cuba owned by US business interests, including a number of large sugar plantations. For a time the huge naval base at Cuba's Guantanamo Bay also seemed threatened. Finally, in January of 1961, the United States broke off diplomatic relations with Cuba.

After Castro's pro-communist, anti-American attitude became clear, the US began to explore ways in which the new Cuban dictator might be overthrown. The importance of the base at Guantanamo plus the fact that Cuba was only some ninety miles from the US mainland made it desirable for a democratic regime sympathetic to American interests to be installed in the key Caribbean island. It was only a matter of time before the possibility of overthrowing Castro was turned over to the CIA. And since Richard Bissell had dealt so effectively with a similar situation in Guatemala, he was put in charge of the new project.

The CIA anti-Castro campaign began in 1960. In March President Eisenhower approved a CIA plan to train two dozen Cuban exiles who had fled Cuba during the revolt of the Fidelistas. Once trained, these men would in turn train other exiles until a hard-hitting revolutionary brigade (La Brigada) was created. Members of La Brigada were to be paid $175 a month plus an additional $50 if they were married, and $25 for each of their children.

La Brigada was actually to overthrow the Castro regime which would be replaced by a new democratic government, called the Frente, which was already forming in Miami. As soon as Castro announced his communist sympathies many of the aides who had helped him overthrow Batista fled from behind Cuba's 'sugar-cane curtain' to Miami. These revolutionaries still believed in a democratic Cuba and helped form the Frente.

Working with the Frente in Miami, which soon resembled a Cuban city, was one of Bissell's aides, a mysterious figure who has never been fully identified but who went by the name of Frank Bender. Bender was soon joined by half a dozen other CIA agents, all operating under assumed names. None admitted any connection with the CIA, claiming instead to be representatives of American companies that had had businesses in Cuba that had been seized by Castro.

From this modest beginning the CIA anti-Castro operation rapidly grew by leaps and bounds until it soon achieved the scale of a major military operation.

The project's growth was a handicap because for diplomatic reasons it was important that the United States government should not be officially connected with plans to overthrow another nation's government. Eisenhower had hoped that if those involved in the operation were all Cuban exiles no blame could be placed on the United States. In addition, it was hoped that while it was still in the planning stages the operation would remain secret. This was to prevent Castro from becoming aware of it.

But as the project grew and more and more people became involved it soon became impossible to limit its participants to ex-Cubans. Military training, for example, had to be supplied by Americans borrowed from the Army and Marine Corps, and ships, aircraft, and other military equipment and supplies had to be furnished by the US as well. Keeping such an operation at the paramilitary level and keeping it secret also became all but an impossibility. Nevertheless, Bissell and his staff proceeded with their project at a breakneck pace, frequently recalling how easily and successfully the Guatemalan operation had been carried out. The idea, of course, was to present Castro with such a large revolutionary threat that he would be panicked into resigning just as Arbenz had done.

Once again Guatemala figured in this plan. It was where the anti-Castro forces were given their military training. A rebel air force flying US B-26 medium bombers and various kinds of fighter aircraft was to be trained and stationed in Nicaragua until D-Day. But unlike the Arbenz government the Castro forces had an excellent combat air force and well-trained army with equipment and supplies furnished by the Soviet Union. One of the reasons Bissell and his aides were so eager to get the operation under way in a hurry was to prevent the Cubans from being supplied with the latest Soviet jet fighter aircraft. As it was, however, the Cubans already had jet trainers that outmatched the propeller-driven planes furnished to La Brigada's air arm.

As his assistants in Washington Bissell had a top-ranking CIA planner and former OSS agent, Tracy Barnes, as well as a Marine Corps Colonel, Jack Hawkins, who was skilled in planning and making amphibious landings on an enemy coast. Hawkins insisted that a minimum of at least 1,400 men would be needed, so what started out as a paramilitary operation finally became a full-scale amphibious military invasion.

There were those people within the CIA who strongly objected to the sheer size of the anti-Castro operation. One of these men was Richard Helms, a top operations officer who later became director of the Agency. Helms had seen reports from CIA agents from within the Cuban exile community in Miami which indicated that the planned invasion was being openly discussed there. There were also rumours about it in both the American and Latin American press. If this were true there was little doubt that Castro's intelligence agency, the Direccion Generale de Inteligencia (DCI), knew all about it as well. But neither Helms nor any other CIA officer raised any open objections that were heard outside the Agency itself, so plans proceeded.

While the Cuban exile troops were in training at a camp called Base Trax in Guatemala, Bissell infiltrated CIA agents into Cuba. These agents – also former Cubans – were supposed to seek out members of the Cuban military as well as those among the general population who opposed the Castro regime and were eager for its overthrow. From among these dissidents the CIA agents were supposed to organize a resistance army that would rise up and aid the invaders on D-Day. The only problem with this plan was that most of the CIA agents were almost immediately captured. In addition, Castro began a round-up of all suspected dissidents on the island and soon had more than 100,000 of them in jail. Despite this initial failure to 'soften up' the island before the invasion, the Bissell plan proceeded. In fact it had taken on something of a life of its own so that probably nothing short of a direct order from President Eisenhower himself could have stopped it.

The plan, however, did not go forward without delay. Training men for the amphibious landing was a slow process. In addition there were delays in obtaining essential support equipment, landing craft and, especially, the B-26 bombers. Eisenhower insisted that the mission, when it became known to the world press, appear to be entirely a Cuban affair. This meant that B-26s had to be 'sold' to various Latin American countries and then acquired by the rebels. Because of this and other delays the invasion was postponed until Eisenhower left office and the newly elected John F. Kennedy was inaugurated president.

If plans for the Cuban invasion had not been at such an advanced stage when Kennedy took office he might well have called it off. But after being briefed by both Dulles and Bissell, who were naturally glowingly optimistic about the prospects for the success of the operation, Kennedy gave it a green light. But like Eisenhower Kennedy was insistent that the operation appear to be of Cuban origin.

As outlined to Kennedy the plans were simple enough. The invasion site was to be at the remote Bay of Pigs. At least two days before the actual landings, air strikes were to be made that would destroy Castro's air force. At dawn on D-Day the area behind the Bay of Pigs was to be 'saturation bombed' by the Nicaragua-based B-26s. Then the amphibious landings were to be made by members of La Brigada who would move inland after crossing the beaches and rapidly fan out. They would be supported by additional B-26 bombers as well as by follow-up waves of troops.

Just who the follow-up waves of troops were to be was never made clear, but leaders of La Brigada later insisted that their American advisors (CIA agents) told them that they would be aided by American troops. Jose Perez San Roman, a La Brigada leader, said bitterly, 'What we were told was, "If you fail, we will go in".' In Miami Manuel Ray of the Frente said, 'We were told that landings would be followed up by all necessary support. We were even told that ten to fifteen thousand men would be available.'

It was also presumed not only by the members of La Brigada but also by Bissell and his Agency colleagues that once a successful amphibious landing had been made there would be a revolt within Castro's army. This never materialized. Bissell was also apparently convinced that once the landings were made the US would be forced to back them up with American troops. This was, to say the least, an unfortunate miscalculation.

There were countless other minor and major miscalculations along the way that led to the final Bay of Pigs fiasco. First and foremost was probably the size and make-up of La Brigada itself. During World War II and the Korean War the US had made numerous successful amphibious landings. But no such major operation had been conducted with fewer than nine battalions of young, highly trained men supported by artillery and complete air superiority. La Brigada was actually the size of *one* US infantry battalion. Its members were partially trained civilians – only a handful were ex-soldiers – averaging about thirty years of age. A few were as old as sixty. Latecomers to La Brigada did not even know how to load or fire a rifle.

Probably the biggest blunder, however, was in the site chosen for the landings. The CIA had chosen the site based on surveys carried out many months earlier. The Bay of Pigs was selected because it was a remote area with deserted beaches where few people ever ventured. But since the survey Castro had decided to turn the area into a public park! Excellent roads now led to several tourist centres. There were also motels, eating places, and bathhouses either built or under construction. The whole waterfront was also gleaming with lights. As historian William Manchester has observed, 'It was as though Russian conspirators had planned a hostile landing on Coney Island.' (Or Brighton.)

But by the time this potentially disastrous situation was discovered the CIA-planned invasion of Cuba was under way.

There was one final mishap that all but guaranteed the failure of the Bay of Pigs operation. In order to divert Castro's attention from the Bay of Pigs another amphibious feint was planned at a distant point in another province, Oriente. This feint was never made because those who were supposed to make it refused to leave their troop ship and board their landing craft. The CIA later blamed 'bad leadership' for this failure, but as historian Manchester has also pointed out, 'The leaders had been chosen by the CIA.'

On Saturday, 15 April 1961, the Bay of Pigs

operation began with an air strike against Castro's air force lined up on the ground at several airfields surrounding Havana. The strike was successful, destroying half of the Cuban planes. What was now needed was an additional strike or strikes so that when the landings were made the invaders would have complete control of the air. No such strikes came.

The first air strike caused immediate world reaction as well as furore in the United Nations. US Ambassador to the United Nations Adlai Stevenson insisted that the United States had played no role in the bombing and was not involved in the rumoured invasion. Stevenson apparently made this statement in good faith, having been assured by other Washington officials that it was true. Later, when Stevenson realized that he too had been used as a CIA pawn, he was furious.

The invasion itself was planned for Monday morning 17 April and all day Sunday Bissell and other CIA aides pleaded with President Kennedy to authorize further air strikes or at least one. But Kennedy flatly refused, insisting that it would be obvious to neutral observers that such air action could only come from the United States.

Nevertheless, on Monday morning the invasion began. Almost immediately a Castro jet trainer sank two of the invasion fleet's ships, including one carrying the rebels' ammunition supply. A further complication arose when it was discovered that the Bay of Pigs was protected by a large coral reef on which the fleet might well founder. US frogmen, despite Kennedy's prohibition against the use of Americans, went into action finding paths through this reef through which the rebel ships could make their way.

Despite spirited opposition from the beach about

three-quarters of the rebels made their way ashore, including a heavy gun battalion. Once ashore members of La Brigada fought heroically and although outnumbered fifteen or twenty to one managed to keep from being overrun. They were under almost constant assault all through the morning.

In Washington Bissell continued to plead with Kennedy to allow additional air strikes. By now Bissell realized the error of his original belief that once the exile Cuban force had landed the US government would be forced to come to its aid. Now Bissell was willing to settle for any aid that would prevent the operation from becoming a rout.

Finally, Kennedy authorized a single air strike for Tuesday morning. But by now the Castro forces, both on land and in the air, were at full alert and three of the B-26s making the second air strike were shot down. Kennedy did take one further step. On Wednesday a US Navy carrier, the *Essex*, just off the coast of Cuba was allowed to provide six unmarked planes for air cover over the Bay of Pigs beaches while the rebel invaders tried to escape. But the timing of the arrival of the Navy's planes was faulty and by Wednesday afternoon those few survivors of the invasion who still remained on the beach surrendered to Castro's troops.

In Washington the reactions to the Bay of Pigs disaster were violent. President Kennedy was in a rage. While he publicly took the blame for the whole affair, privately he threatened to abolish the CIA. Finally he simply settled for the resignations of Allen Dulles and Richard Bissell. They were replaced by John McCone and Richard Helms, the latter having been the one major CIA figure who had opposed the Bay of Pigs operation from the beginning.

But the changes in top leadership at the CIA did not wipe the slate clean with Cuba. Kennedy and the CIA were to be involved with Cuba and Castro right up to the day of the youthful president's assassination, and there were those who thought that Castro may also have been involved in that dark deed.

6
Dark and bloody deeds

There is little doubt that the time period between the founding of the CIA and the Bay of Pigs debacle was the Agency's golden era. Between 1947 and 1961 the CIA went more or less quietly about its business gathering intelligence and accomplishing the clandestine jobs with which it was charged. To be sure, the shooting down of Gary Powers in his spy plane in 1960 created a break in this smooth pattern of operations, but it was rather quickly forgotten by the American public.

The truth of the matter was that the American public did not really want to know what the CIA was up to. Most people wished there did not have to be such an organization but more or less accepted the fact that it was a necessity in the modern world. But even if the CIA were a necessary evil people wished it would simply go about its business secretly the way it was supposed to and not make them aware of and thus partially responsible for the dirty business of spying and clandestine operations.

The Bay of Pigs began to change all that. Obviously the CIA and thus the United States had made fools of themselves in an operation in which they probably had no business taking part in the first place. There wasn't much of a chance that the Bay of Pigs could be hidden or forgotten about. The Soviets and Soviet sympathizers were not about to let that happen no matter how much the US government, the CIA and the American public wished they would. Consequently, from the Bay of Pigs right up to the present day the CIA has been pretty much fair game for the American public's criticism.

Despite the criticism, the CIA continued to try and do its job and, as many of the Agency's defenders have pointed out, for the most part it did it well. One of the problems, of course, with clandestine operations is that when they are done well the public does not hear about them. This is the hallmark of a good secret agent and the espionage agency he/she works for. A successful intelligence operation is never reported in the newspapers or on television. An unsuccessful one makes media headlines and is telecast around the world.

The Cuban missile crisis

One exception to this rule occurred in October of 1962 and once again had to do with Cuba. In October of that year the United States learned that installations for launching long-range nuclear missiles were being installed on the island. The discovery was made by one of the CIA's high altitude spy planes overflying Cuba. When President Kennedy announced this fact to the American public – and the world – he did so on television. As part of his presentation the president showed actual photographs of the missile launchers taken by the spy plane. The photographs were clear as crystal and left no doubt in anybody's mind about what the Cubans and their Soviet allies were up to.

In case there *was* any doubt Kennedy pointed out that the CIA had also learned that Castro had requested Russia to install the missile launchers as well as rockets equipped with nuclear warheads in Cuba. Now, Kennedy said, he was demanding that the rocket-launching installations be immediately removed.

The challenge reached its climax when Kennedy ordered the Navy to intercept Soviet ships carrying rockets for the installations. This quarantine was accompanied by an ultimatum to the Soviet Union stating that if Cuba attacked the United States, the United States would instantly unleash its nuclear arsenal against Russia.

For a dark and terrible moment the world stood poised on the brink of nuclear war. Millions of Americans watched on television as rocket-laden Soviet ships approached Cuba and the US Navy prepared to intercept them. For terrifyingly long hours the United States and the Soviet Union stood eyeball to eyeball. And then the Russians blinked. Soviet Premier Nikita Khrushchev ordered the Russian ships to turn back. He also ordered the dismantling of the missile installations already erected in Cuba, and the missiles that were already there were to be returned to the Soviet Union. The world breathed a terrible sigh of relief at the narrow escape from nuclear annihilation.

'Murder Inc. in the Caribbean'

After the missile crisis died down and a degree of calm was restored in the Caribbean both President Kennedy and the CIA continued to scheme about how to get rid of Castro. One of the ugliest if most decisive methods considered was to assassinate the Cuban leader.

All during the brief Kennedy Administration there were rumours that the president himself had approved such drastic action. But such rumours have never been proved. There is no doubt, however, that Kennedy considered the idea. In November 1961 the president asked reporter Tad Szculc, 'How would you feel if the United States assassinated Castro?' Szculc said he thought that was a poor idea, and Kennedy replied, 'I'm glad you feel that way because suggestions to that effect keep coming to me, and I believe very strongly the United States should not be a party to political assassination.'

Apparently the CIA had no misgivings about not only considering the idea but also acting on it. And following President Kennedy's assassination in Dallas in November of 1963 several high government officials speculated that his death was in retaliation for approving CIA efforts to kill Castro. In fact Kennedy's successor, President Lyndon Johnson, even blurted to newsmen, 'Kennedy tried to get Castro but Castro got Kennedy first.' Later Johnson tried to retract this statement but went on to say, 'They were running a damned Murder Inc. in the Caribbean.'

Johnson's latter statement, in part at least, referred to the assassination of another dictator, Rafael Trujillo of the Dominican Republic, on 30 May 1961. Rumour had it that the CIA had supplied the guns to

Dominican dissidents for this murder, although once again this rumour has never been fully substantiated.

Another assassination of a foreign leader in which the CIA was said to have been directly involved was that of Patrice Lumumba of the former Belgian Congo (today's Zaire), also in 1961. Lumumba had been poisoned by Congolese tribesmen, but the rumour went that they had been encouraged to do so by CIA agents. In addition, former CIA station chief John Stockwell has reported that after the murder in Lubumbashi a CIA officer had told Stockwell about 'driving around town after curfew with Patrice Lumumba's body in the trunk of his car, trying to decide what to do with it.'

Whether or not President Kennedy or members of his administration such as his brother Robert ever called upon the CIA to kill Castro will probably never be known. It should be noted, however, that the CIA does not act without authorization from the president. In addition, such authorization would certainly never be in writing. Further, in general discussions about Castro it might simply have been 'understood' that the elimination of Castro would not be disapproved by the White House.

'Operation Mongoose'

In any event it is known that the CIA did plan to kill Castro. This plan was called 'Operation Mongoose'.

In 1966 Congress passed the Freedom of Information Act. This gave the public access to a wide range of once-secret documents. Using this Act as a lever, investigative reporters soon learned that an organization aimed at plotting counter-revolution in Cuba in general and killing Castro in particular had been formed following the Bay of Pigs. Heading Operation Mongoose was General Edward G. Lansdale, a legendary counter-revolution specialist who had already had experience organizing such movements in both the Philippines and Vietnam.

Lansdale's original plan called for a march on Havana following the infiltration of rebel bands of guerrillas into Cuba. The march was to take place in October of 1962. Before then a network of CIA spies was to be set up throughout the island. These spies were supposed to organize sabotage operations, including the blowing up of important Cuban mining installations, sugar refineries, and oil storage depots.

Meanwhile, the CIA also secretly enlisted organized crime to kill Castro. The crime syndicate itself was keenly interested in getting rid of the Cuban dictator so it could re-establish its gambling operations in Cuba which Castro had driven out when he took over control of the country.

Sam Giancana, a Chicago crime boss, was one of the go-betweens used by the CIA to arrange attempts on Castro's life. (The FBI apparently knew of these arrangements, but it, too, kept them secret until Congress forced their disclosure.) The assassination plans rivalled anything author Ian Fleming ever dreamed up for his hero James Bond. They included a poisoned cigar that was to be slipped into the inveterate cigar-smoking Cuban leader's supply of high-priced Havana specials; a wet-suit impregnated with deadly germs that Castro wore when going scuba diving; and an explosives-filled giant clam shell that Castro would step on when he waded into the water at his favourite beach.

All of these plans were abandoned when it became

clear that they could not be carried out without the mischance that somebody other than Castro might accidentally become the victim. There is little doubt, however, that some such plan was put into operation because in a July 1973 *Atlantic Monthly* magazine article Leo Janos, a former Lyndon Johnson aide, wrote, 'A year or so before Kennedy's death a CIA-backed assassination team had been picked up in Havana.' In addition, Castro had obviously learned about plans to kill him because he referred to them in public broadcasts heard in the United States.

Following President Kennedy's assassination, the Lansdale march on Havana was also called off by President Johnson. Involved in the Vietnam War, Johnson was never much interested in Cuba. But the question remained in Johnson's and many other people's minds – had Castro struck against President Kennedy before he himself could be killed? Castro always stoutly and convincingly denied this, and realistic observers pointed out that the Cuban dictator would have had little to gain and much to lose by risking bringing down the wrath of the mighty United States on his tiny nation's head through such a venture. But if Castro had taken just such a risk in inviting the Soviet Union to install nuclear missiles in Cuba, why would he hesitate to eliminate his arch foe, President John F. Kennedy?

Assassin's bizarre background

A further nagging doubt regarding the Kennedy assassination and its possible Cuban connection that has plagued researchers, has had to do with the accused assassin himself, Lee Harvey Oswald. To say the least, Oswald had a bizarre background. An ex-US Marine, Oswald had actually lived for a time in the Soviet Union. He was also known to have made a lengthy visit to Cuba and was not only a communist sympathizer but also a staunch supporter of Fidel Castro. These facts have led some writers to claim that Oswald was part of a communist plot co-sponsored by the Soviet Union and Cuba to kill Kennedy. Other writers have implied that Oswald was actually a double agent, supposedly a member of the CIA or FBI hired to spy on Castro's supporters in the United States, but actually a Castro agent sent to the United States by Cuba's intelligence agency, the Direccion Generale de Inteligencia, to eliminate the US president.

It should be pointed out that after each assassination or attempted assassination of an American president – and they have been frequent – invariably wild rumours and stories of national or international conspiracies have sprung up regarding the murders.

Other presidential assassinations and assassination attempts

Since the end of the American Civil War one out of every five United States presidents has been assassinated. They were Abraham Lincoln, James A. Garfield, William McKinley and John F. Kennedy. During that same period attempts have also been made on the lives of five other chief executives, Theodore Roosevelt, Franklin D. Roosevelt, Harry S. Truman, Gerald Ford (twice), and Ronald Reagan. Earlier, on 30 January 1835, an attempt was also made to kill President Andrew Jackson. This was the first attempt on the life of a United States president.

In most instances the motives of the assassins and would-be assassins were at first generally accepted by the public at face value – mentally twisted though the motives might be. Actor John Wilkes Booth, Lincoln's assassin, was a Southern sympathizer who hated Lincoln because of the outcome of the Civil War. Charles J. Guiteau, the man who killed Garfield, was a disappointed office seeker. Anarchist Leon F. Czolgosz, McKinley's killer, was politically motivated and perhaps simply insane with an urge to kill a 'great ruler'. Would-be assassins Richard Lawrence (Jackson), John Schrank (Teddy Roosevelt), Guiseppe Zangara (FDR), and Oscar Galazo and Griselio Torresola (Truman) were all misguided political idealists, clearly insane, or both. Lynette 'Squeaky' Fromme, who was seized for aiming a pistol at Gerald Ford, was a mentally warped follower of the Charles Manson murder cult, and Sara Jane Moore, who later actually fired a revolver at Ford, was a misguided political activist. Both were mentally unstable. John W. Hinckley, Jr., who shot and wounded Ronald Reagan as well as several others in the Reagan group outside a Washington hotel, was actually committed to a mental hospital.

The Warren Report

After all of these presidential assassinations and attempted assassinations investigations were carried on at the highest government level, usually by the Secret Service. In the case of the Kennedy assassination, Kennedy's successor, Lyndon Johnson, appointed a high-level commission headed by the chief justice of the Supreme Court to thoroughly investigate the assassination and to present all of the facts to the American people.

Serving on the Warren Commission was ex-CIA Director Allen Dulles, and the investigation was given the full support of the CIA, the FBI, and the Secret Service. In addition there were several senators and congressmen, including Gerald Ford who would himself later become president and have assassination attempts made on his life. John J. McCloy, one of President Kennedy's former top advisors, gave Chief Justice Warren valuable assistance, and ex-United States Solicitor General James Lee Rankin was the Commission's chief counsel.

The Warren Commission actually began its investigation in February of 1964. During the next eight months it heard more than 550 witnesses and examined countless pieces of evidence as well as photographs relating to the slaying. In late September the Commission issued a one-volume report which was followed by twenty-six volumes of testimony, photographs, and other exhibits.

The Warren Report's conclusion was that Lee Harvey Oswald, for reasons not known, acted alone in killing President Kennedy. There was no indication of international involvement with Cuba, the Soviet Union or any other country, and no hint that Oswald had ever had any CIA connections.

For a time after the Warren Report was issued the nation's doubts were stilled. Then the doubts and wonderings began all over again. Various investigative journalists – some of them sincere, responsible truth-seekers, and others irresponsible sensation-seekers – began to find flaws in the Warren Report. Some even said the Report was a massive government cover-up of what had actually happened and who was really responsible. Oswald had never confessed to the crime. If he had committed it alone and unsponsored, what was his motive?

These doubts have persisted to the present day. So have the investigations. But if the CIA has any additional information on the subject that information has not been publicly disclosed. As is its custom, the CIA has not said an additional word.

7
The CIA invades the 'Halls of Ivy'

After remaining out of the headlines for several years the CIA again became the centre of controversy in 1967. This occurred when the magazine *Ramparts* published several articles in its February issue disclosing that the CIA had invaded hundreds of American colleges and universities beginning as far back as 1952.

For some years it had been rumoured that the CIA was secretly subsidizing certain private foundations, research centres, and book publishers. In the publishing industry, for example, it was more or less common knowledge that one publisher was being kept in business with CIA subsidies that paid the cost of producing certain propaganda-type books that the Agency wanted published. But until the *Ramparts* disclosures it was not generally known that the CIA had also invaded the 'Halls of Ivy' on a vast scale.

Ramparts declared that for nearly fifteen years the CIA had been financing the foreign programmes of the National Student Association (NSA). The NSA was an organization managed by students in more than 300 American colleges and universities. During that period the CIA had poured some $3 million into the NSA treasury and had helped pay for the organization's headquarters building in Washington, D.C.

The CIA's purpose in invading the nation's colleges and universities was twofold. First of all, there were a number of foreign students studying at these schools. Once the CIA was made welcome on certain campuses easy access to these foreign students was made possible. And once the foreign students were befriended the CIA could go about its business of recruiting them as secret agents who would go to work for the Agency when they returned to their homelands.

Secondly, and probably of greater importance, the CIA wanted young Americans who travelled abroad as representatives of the NSA at various international youth conferences to be indoctrinated with the 'proper' pro-United States, anti-Soviet Union attitudes. For this indoctrination the CIA had established a special division known as the Department of Psychological, Political, and Paramilitary Programs. Since, according to the CIA, these international youth organizations were Red Front groups strongly represented by foreign communist youths, it was in the best American interests to have United States representatives be not merely non-communist but also anti-communist. The CIA also provided funds for the establishment of non-communist youth organizations in many of the Third World or underdeveloped nations.

Tied in with this Cold War effort in the developing nations, although not referred to in the *Ramparts* articles, was an early effort by the CIA to infiltrate its agents into the Peace Corps. The Peace Corps had been a pet project of John Kennedy's as early as 1960. Established in 1961, its purpose was to provide people trained in a variety of skills to help countries in need.

Although there was no upper age limit placed on the first Peace Corps volunteers, its emphasis was on young people who could pass a rigorous physical examination. When it was first established, the Peace Corps was an agency of the State Department. This made it seem like an ideal cover for CIA agents, just as other State Department agencies provided. This thought also occurred to the Soviets, who immediately denounced the Peace Corps as an American espionage operation.

But despite efforts of CIA agents to infiltrate the Peace Corps such an opportunity was denied them. Both R. Sargent Shriver, its early director, and President Kennedy himself flatly refused such use of their pet project. In 1971 the Peace Corps was removed from State Department control and absorbed by an independent government agency known as ACTION. So far as is known the Peace Corps continues to be free of CIA spies.

The *Ramparts* articles renewed public demands for the congressional investigation of the CIA, and there were also demands in some quarters that the Agency be abolished. Responding to this criticism, President Johnson ordered that all CIA financing of the National Student Association be suspended. He also authorized an investigation of all secret subsidy programmes by the federal government.

During the course of the investigations many surprising facts were discovered. It was learned, for example, that no less an institution than the Massachusetts Institute of Technology had been directly involved with the CIA. This was through MIT's Center for International Studies whose founding had been partly financed by the Agency. Just how much money MIT had received was not learned, but it was disclosed that another school, Michigan State University, had received some $25 million to provide cover for secret CIA overseas operations.

Various private foundations, it was also learned, had received CIA financing. These included the Asia Foundation, the Congress of Cultural Freedom and a host of others. In addition, several labour, church, and philanthropic organizations offering technical assistance to foreign countries had also long been used as CIA cover.

Among many conservative Americans it had long been suspected that a number of these organizations had already been infiltrated by communists. Why then, they asked, wasn't it fair to infiltrate them with pro-American agents? Generally, however, the CIA subsidy of these groups was frowned upon. At the heart of the criticism of such activity by the CIA was the threat it offered to traditionally free American educational and private institutions. Such subversive and covert activity within American colleges and universities, critics said, threatened the democratic spirit of free inquiry and risked turning the nation's schools into government-controlled pawns in the Cold War. What was the point, these critics asked, in fighting a cold war against totalitarianism if in the process one destroyed the American free society?

Scholars and scientists also resented not knowing whether their research was truly free and honest research or whether it was being conducted to serve political ends. Church leaders and heads of philanthropic organizations opposed perverting altruistic efforts into secret means of gaining government goals.

In the end President Johnson agreed with the findings of federal investigators that 'no federal agency shall provide any covert financial assistance to support, direct or indirect, any of the nation's educational or private voluntary organizations'.

Gradually, American colleges and universities got out of the subsidized spy business but irreparable harm had been done to many of them and the CIA image had been further tarnished. As a consequence of this experience and CIA activity during the Vietnam War, CIA recruiting became less and less welcome on college and university campuses. This attitude has continued up to the present day. As recently as the mid-1980s, for example, there were student demonstrations on the Northwestern University campus in Evanston, Illinois, when CIA recruiters arrived there and an attempt was made to prevent them from interviewing prospective CIA candidates. Such demonstrations have also frequently occurred elsewhere throughout the United States.

It should be noted that the CIA never has any serious problems with hiring new employees. In fact quite the reverse is true. The Agency receives a quarter of a million job applications a year, so it can well afford to pick and choose among the best and the brightest.

In addition, the CIA carries on an open and above board arrangement with some eighty colleges which it calls the 'Cooperative Education Program'. Actually this is a work-study programme in which participating students may work six months for the CIA in Washington or at Langley and then spend six months on campus.

The CIA reinvades the campuses

When Richard Nixon succeeded Lyndon Johnson as president in January 1969, he made it perfectly clear that he did not think much of the CIA, mainly because he felt they never got anything accomplished in their anti-communist efforts. 'All you've got is forty thousands people over there reading newspapers,' Nixon once commented to an aide regarding the Agency. Nixon, of course, had made his name politically as a red-hunter during his early years in Congress.

Nevertheless, Nixon, like every president since Truman, felt free to call upon the CIA for numerous clandestine chores. One of these was to ask the CIA to determine if there was a connection between the Soviet Union and unrest and anti-Vietnam War activity on the nation's college campuses. Actually, this should have been an FBI job since the FBI is charged with interior US activities and the CIA with exterior activity, but the FBI seemed reluctant to do anything about heeding Nixon's requests in this area. Finally, the CIA took on the task under what was known as 'Operation Chaos'.

Operation Chaos was intended to cover the whole domestic scene to determine if various groups protesting against the war in Vietnam were being spurred into action by international communism. But since most of the protest groups were youths of college age the operation once again invaded the campuses. This time it did so in a clandestine way by attempting to recruit college students as spies to report on their classmates.

It should be made clear that within the CIA itself there was much strong feeling against Operation

Chaos. Those who objected to it felt that not only did it violate the CIA charter which prohibited domestic operations, but it also violated certain long-held beliefs about the invasion of privacy in American society. Nevertheless, Richard Helms, who by this time was in charge of the CIA, attempted to do Nixon's bidding and as the anti-Vietnam War movement grew so did Operation Chaos.

The only problem was that Operation Chaos produced few important results, or at least few results of the kind the Nixon administration sought. Helms' reports consistently showed that student dissidence was a worldwide activity and in the United States it was particularly active because of the drafting of young men for military service in Vietnam. The anti-Vietnam War atmosphere continued to grow more and more violent as the conflict progressed, and American students needed no outside prompting to demonstrate against it. Rather than being influenced by international communism the general revolt of American young people was quite obviously a home-grown affair.

Eventually Operation Chaos collapsed in the 1970s, both because of lack of results as well as because of strong objections to it by FBI Director J. Edgar Hoover. Hoover did not object to trying to track down communists on the domestic scene – communism and its infiltration into American life was an obsession with him – but he *did* object to the CIA trying to take over FBI turf which he guarded zealously.

Meanwhile, while there may have been dissension within CIA ranks regarding Operation Chaos, there was certainly no dissension about CIA operations in Southeast Asia during the Vietnam War. There the

CIA joined ranks and carried on what amounted to a full-scale clandestine military effort. Eventually that effort was to play a key role in the tragic loss of the Vietnam War by the United States.

8
The CIA in the Vietnam War

The Cold War between the Soviet Union and the United States spilled over into Southeast Asia in the mid-1950s. This was when the French were driven out of Vietnam by communist North Vietnam forces. At an international peace conference in Geneva, Switzerland, following the French defeat, it was decided to temporarily divide Vietnam into two parts, North and South Vietnam. North Vietnam was to belong to the communist government headed by Ho Chi Minh. South Vietnam was to be a republic with, it was hoped, a democratic form of government. Eventually there were to be nationwide elections to reunite the country and decide who would run it. Since the United States wanted to prevent the spread of communism throughout Southeast Asia it naturally backed South Vietnam and its president, Ngo Dinh Diem.

Almost immediately President Dwight Eisenhower began sending military aid and military advisors to support Diem's South Vietnamese army. At first this aid was a mere trickle and the advisors amounted to only a few hundred men. But under several successive American presidents, Kennedy, Johnson and Nixon, the aid became a flood and the number of military men eventually swelled to more than half a million. Soon the United States was actually fighting the war and not merely giving advice on how it should be conducted. Eventually it would become the longest conflict in American history and the first war the United States had ever lost.

Among the first advisors to arrive in South Vietnam were several CIA agents. They were supposed to advise the president on the political situation in South Vietnam. Soon the handful of CIA agents, like the American military aid, swelled to a flood that numbered more than a thousand. These CIA agents in turn hired several thousand contract employees. This CIA operation was run under the cover of the embassy in Saigon, the capital of South Vietnam, as the Office of Special Assistance. Before many months the CIA was conducting its own secret war in Southeast Asia.

The CIA's first major act, however, was to take part in the overthrow of South Vietnam's President Diem. Diem proved to be a dictator who was not interested in holding any kind of elections that might remove him from power. Several members of the State Department plus CIA Director Richard Helms finally agreed that the Diem regime must be overthrown. Approval for the coup, which took place on 1 November 1963, was given by President Kennedy. Kennedy did not approve of what followed.

Diem and his brother Nhu were physically removed from their offices in Saigon by dissident South Vietnamese generals who were probably encouraged to act by the CIA. Shortly after their removal the Diem brothers were found slain. President Kennedy was visibly upset when he heard this news, but few CIA officers were sympathetic with his reactions. Their general feeling was that the president had approved the coup and should have known what probably would happen.

Two weeks later Kennedy himself was killed and among the rumours surrounding his death was one that said it was somehow tied in with the Diem assassination. No connection between the slayings has ever been established.

The CIA army in Laos

As the United States became more and more active in the Vietnam War so did the CIA. One of the CIA's first moves was to organize an army of Meo tribesmen and women in neighbouring Laos. The role of this army was to disrupt traffic from North Vietnam into South Vietnam along the Ho Chi Minh Trail.

Beginning with a few Meo guerrillas in 1962, the CIA expanded this operation into a thirty-thousand man and woman army by the late 1960s. As the Meo threat grew so did the North Vietnamese reaction to it. What started out as a minor guerrilla action soon developed into full-scale warfare between the Meos and North Vietnamese military forces. In the end, as the United States gradually began to withdraw from the war, the Meos were left to fend for themselves. The result was the virtual destruction of not only the Meo military forces but also the Meos as a people. As historian Thomas Powers has pointed out, 'Of perhaps a quarter of a million Meos in 1962, only a pitiful remnant of ten thousand escaped to Thailand in 1975.' But the war in Laos was always regarded as a CIA success, perhaps because it was fought at a cost of only $20 million to $30 million a year – a fraction of the cost of the war in Vietnam itself.

Other tribesmen and women whom the CIA organized to combat the North Vietnamese were the Montagnards in Vietnam's central highland region. The Special Forces or Green Berets actually commanded the Montagnards under CIA guidance. This effort was somewhat more successful than that of the Meos in Laos until the Montagnards demanded that they be allowed to operate as an independent army. At this point the CIA relinquished control of the Montagnards to the US Army.

Eventually, of course, the heroic Montagnards were totally abandoned by all American forces and allowed to starve or be captured or killed by the North Vietnamese. As CIA Vietnamese veteran John Stockwell has said, 'At the end in Vietnam I had participated in an evacuation in which the CIA leaders had fled in panic, abandoning people whom we had recruited and exposed in our operations ... Very little about CIA activity in Vietnam was honourable.'

The Phoenix Program

Perhaps the most notorious CIA operation in Vietnam was the Phoenix Program which resulted in the deaths of somewhere between 20,000 and 40,000 people, depending upon who was doing the counting. Headed by future CIA Director William Colby, Phoenix was supposedly a pacification programme. Actually it was a counter-terror programme aimed at fighting the Vietcong by using the Vietcong's own terror tactics. The Vietcong was the name given to forces in Vietnam who were loyal to North Vietnam.

During the course of the war it grew more and more difficult to tell which people in South Vietnam *were* loyal to the South Vietnamese Republic and which ones were actually loyal to North Vietnam. The Phoenix Program was aimed at seeking out those subversives as well as actual Vietcong military leaders. Identification was made mainly by kidnapping suspects, taking them to local interrogation centres and torturing them to confess. Once they confessed they were executed. Agency Director Colby later told Congress that more than 20,000 suspected Vietcong were killed during the two and a half years of the Phoenix Program. South Vietnamese officials set the figure at more than 40,000.

One of the main problems with the Phoenix Program was that of actually identifying members of the Vietcong. Suspects were not infrequently dishonestly named by people wanting to gain favour with the Americans. Other informers acted out of spite or desire for revenge. Occasionally such suspects were not even taken to interrogation centres but merely caught in their homes and shot, not infrequently while they were still asleep. Sometimes raids were made on villages where suspects were said to be living and these raids resulted in fire-fights in which innocent men, women and children were killed.

The order of battle dispute

As the Vietnam War progressed and the United States seemed unable to gain a victory, the CIA and the military became involved in a bitter dispute over the actual number of enemy who opposed the United States and South Vietnamese forces. The CIA reported that the enemy order of battle or number of combat troops totalled between 500,000 and 600,000 men.

But General William Westmoreland, the US commander in Vietnam, insisted that this number should be no more than 300,000 and that the extra 200,000-plus that the CIA was reporting were civilian non-combatants, not soldiers. These were called Vietcong irregulars or self-defence and secret self-defence militias.

All during the Vietnam War the American forces were plagued with apparent civilians who suddenly turned into grenade-carrying, knife-wielding enemies when they were approached. The fact that many of these enemy 'civilians' were also women and children made the task of fighting the Vietcong a nightmarish affair. Evidently it was somewhere in this shadowy area of who was an enemy soldier and who was an innocent, non-combatant civilian that the difference between the CIA order of battle figure and that of the Army top command occurred. Eventually the CIA agreed to accept the Army's estimate and the matter apparently died there.

But after the war, rumours began to surface that the Westmoreland command had actually falsified the number of enemy troops so that the American public and Congress would not become alarmed. If the enemy order of battle were suddenly to jump by some 200,000 men it would appear, so the rumours went, that the United States was actually losing the war and not winning it. This might well add fuel to the anti-war fires that were already burning so furiously in the United States.

Rumours about the doctored enemy troop strength surfaced in a number of postwar magazine articles and books. Then, in 1982, the Columbia Broadcasting System's *Sixty Minutes* television programme presented a segment claiming that there had actually been a 'conspiracy' on the part of General Westmoreland and his command to prevent the original CIA order of battle figures from being made public during the war. A short time later Westmoreland sued CBS for libel. Also sued was Sam Adams, a former CIA officer in Vietnam who had left the Agency after the war, and who had acted as a consultant for the CBS conspiracy programme.

Suddenly, as the lengthy trial neared its end in mid-February of 1985, General Westmoreland decided to withdraw his $120 million lawsuit. The decision was reached when testimony appeared to neutral observers to be going against the general, especially that testimony offered by retired Army Colonel Gains B. Hawkins, who was the chief of the order of battle or roster of enemy troop estimates in Vietnam. Hawkins said that when he brought General Westmoreland a higher enemy troop total in 1967, Westmoreland said the figures were 'politically unacceptable'. Actually, however, neither CBS nor Westmoreland 'won' any trial verdict, both sides agreeing that 'history would be the final judge'.

The Pentagon Papers

During the late 1960s when the Vietnam War was at its height, US Secretary of Defence Robert S. McNamara had his staff at the Pentagon prepare a secret report on just how the United States had become involved in the conflict and how it had been conducted up to that point.

One of the people who worked on the report was a young man named Daniel Ellsberg. Ellsberg opposed the Vietnam War and thought the US was mainly to blame for it. The Pentagon report seemed to prove his belief, and he thought it should be published. Despite their secret classification, Ellsberg decided to leak the so-called 'Pentagon Papers' to the press.

The Pentagon Papers were first printed in the *New York Times* beginning on 13 June 1971. Later they were published in the *Washington Post* and elsewhere despite the attempt by the Nixon administration to stop their publication. The Supreme Court ruled that the publication of the documents was permitted under the First Amendment to the Constitution. Ellsberg was also arrested and indicted for violating the American Espionage Act but was acquitted after an eighty-nine day trial.

The Pentagon Papers left little to the imagination. They showed how several presidents had got the nation more and more deeply involved in Indochina. Many undercover activities, even before the US had become actually involved in the conflict, were disclosed. The combat activities of the Green Berets and the secret operations of the CIA were now made public for the first time. Detailed accounts of the secret CIA army's action in Laos were given. Also disclosed was the fact that CIA reports indicated that the aerial bombing of Hanoi, capital of North Vietnam, only made North Vietnam more determined than ever to continue the war. Yet such bombings had continued, so the CIA's one constructive contribution to the conflict had been in vain.

At the time the Pentagon Papers were published it was generally agreed that they were far more critical of Lyndon Johnson than they were of Richard Nixon who succeeded Johnson as president. The reason the Nixon administration tried to suppress them was because it wanted to prevent any similar secret reports on Nixon's own undercover efforts from being published in the future. Nixon also took another fatal step. He ordered his aides to break into the office of a psychiatrist Ellsberg had consulted in Los Angeles, Dr Lewis J. Fielding. These burglars were called the 'Plumbers' Unit' because they were supposed to fix the leak of any more government secrets. The Plumbers hoped to find information about Ellsberg that might hurt his reputation.

Interestingly, among the members of the original Plumbers' Unit that broke into Dr Fielding's office were E. Howard Hunt, a former CIA agent, and Eugenio Martinez, a Cuban exile and veteran of Operation Mongoose who was still being paid $100 a month by the CIA as a part-time contract employee. Through his former Agency connections Hunt was able to get technical assistance – a camera and a disguise – from the CIA for use in the break-in, but it has never been proved that the CIA ever had any direct connection with the Fielding burglary.

Actually the burglary of Dr Fielding's office in the fall of 1971 accomplished nothing as far as disclosing any negative information about Ellsberg. But it was a significant first move on the part of the infamous Plumbers' Unit which was to be involved in the notorious Watergate break-in the following spring.

The Watergate Affair

On Saturday night, 17 June 1972, a second Plumbers' Unit broke into the headquarters of the Democratic National Committee in the Watergate Hotel and office complex in Washington D.C. This was during a national election campaign and the Plumbers were attempting to plant 'bugs' or wiretaps in the phones of President Richard Nixon's political opponents and also to steal documents that might disclose his opponents' campaign plans. The Plumbers were caught in the midst of their attempted burglary by an alert night watchman who called the police. They were not immediately linked to Nixon and his aides, however, and Nixon went on to win his overwhelming victory over George McGovern, the Democratic candidate for the presidency.

Three of the five burglars were soon identified as having CIA connections. They were Hunt and Martinez, who had taken part in the Dr Fielding burglary, and James McCord, a former top-level CIA security officer. Neither Hunt nor McCord was still connected with the Agency, but Martinez was still on his retainer. The Martinez CIA connection was ended the day after the Watergate break-in.

Actually the Watergate affair did not become headline news for many months because no link between the burglary and the Nixon administration was established until 1974. Then it became known that President Nixon had learned of the Watergate break-in shortly after it happened and had immediately ordered a cover-up of the burglary. During the course of the Watergate disclosures it also became known that Nixon's aides had planned and carried out the earlier burglary of Ellsberg's psychiatrist's office. Faced with impeachment because of his participation in the Watergate affair, Nixon resigned as president on 8 August 1974, and was succeeded by Gerald Ford.

During the course of the lengthy Watergate hearings and afterwards it was suggested by White House aides Charles Colson, H. R. Haldeman and others that the CIA had actually planned the Watergate break-in.

Agency Director Richard Helms flatly denied this before a Congressional investigating committee and has denied it ever since. Investigative reporters have been inclined to support Helms, although there still remains some doubt about whether Nixon and his aides were solely responsible for one of the most disgraceful episodes in American history. Some of the doubts were raised by the fact that early in 1973, while Nixon was still in office, Richard Helms was suddenly relieved as director of the CIA and given the post of ambassador to Iran. But Helm's firing may well be attributed to his refusal to go along with the Nixon administration's plan to have the CIA take responsibility for the Watergate break-in and the subsequent cover-up.

9
The 'family jewels'

Richard Helms was highly respected by his CIA colleagues for the fact that he never told *any* Agency secrets. He lived up to this reputation when he underwent Senate Foreign Relations Committee confirmation hearings as ambassador to Iran in February 1973. But some of his answers on this occasion were eventually to get Helms into serious trouble.

Helms' replies came to several questions asked seemingly out of the blue by Senator Stuart Symington.

'Did you try in the Central Intelligence Agency to overthrow the government of Chile?' Symington asked.

'No, sir,' Helms said.

'Did you have money passed to the opponents of Allende?' Symington asked.

'No, sir,' Helms said.

To other similar queries Helms gave either a flat 'no' or was evasive in his replies.

But the truth of the matter was that the CIA *had* been involved in trying to overthrow the government of Chile. What was more the CIA had also been at least indirectly involved in the assassination of

General René Schneider, Commander of the Chilean Armed Forces.

Helms' testimony and other testimony he gave later along similar lines lay quietly buried in Senate files until early September 1974 when Seymour Hersh broke a story in the *New York Times* revealing earlier CIA clandestine activities in Chile. Hersh was a Pulitzer Prize-winning reporter for his dispatches during the Vietnam War so his CIA story commanded attention.

Soon the Senate Select Committee headed by Senator Frank Church was busily investigating all US intelligence activities, and in 1975 it released a preliminary report confirming the Hersh story. Surprisingly, this activity in Chile had apparently begun as far back as 1963 and had continued right up until 1973 when Helms left the Agency. The major CIA activity in Chile, however, had occurred during the Nixon Administration when Helms was still at the CIA helm. Details of this activity were as follows:

In October of 1970 Salvador Allende had been scheduled to take part in a three-way run-off election for the Chilean presidency, an election that pollsters agreed he would probably win. A widely recognized political leftist, Allende was believed to be secretly supported by the Soviet Union and communist Cuba. In fact after he left office, Nixon recalled in a television interview with David Frost the following incident that took place just before the Chilean election: 'An Italian businessman came to call on me in the Oval Office, and he said, "If Allende should win the election in Chile, and then you have Castro in Cuba, what you will have in effect in Latin America is a red sandwich and eventually it will all be red."'

Determined not to let the Soviets gain a foothold in

Chile, Nixon decided to make an all-out effort to prevent Allende from being elected. He did this by calling upon both the State Department and the CIA to mount a propaganda campaign to prevent Allende's election. When this brought no apparent results, Nixon and his aides went a step further and ordered CIA Director Helms and the Agency to prevent Allende from taking office.

In commenting on this order in his book *Facing Reality*, former CIA officer Cord Meyer later wrote, 'In retrospect, it is possible that we could have forced a reconsideration of this decision by a unanimous act of protest, but the respect for presidential authority ran too deep, and we did not even consider the alternative.'

Instead, the CIA set about trying to carry out Nixon's order by getting the Chilean military to take part in a coup to overthrow Allende. Army Commander General Schneider was the chief obstacle. He was a firm believer in following Chilean constitutional law and would have no part in military interference with a duly elected official. Knowing that Schneider commanded great respect throughout Chile, the CIA prepared to drop the idea of a coup. But another Chilean officer, a General Romero Viaux, and a small group of plotters – acting on their own according to the CIA – went ahead and attempted to kidnap General Schneider. While resisting the kidnap attempt, General Schneider was killed.

The Schneider murder solidified support for Allende, and he took office and remained in power until September of 1973. Then another group of Chilean officers moved against Allende, assassinating him and driving his government from office. According to the Church Committee's report, 'Neither the US

Embassy nor the CIA was involved in Allende's overthrow.' As ex-CIA officer Meyer has observed, however, 'It could be argued that Nixon's attempt to stimulate a coup in 1970 may have made a lasting impression on some of the Chilean officers.'

It was these findings by the Church Committee – and also by the House of Representatives' own Select Committee later established with Otis Pike as chairman – that came back to haunt Richard Helms. Asked by the Department of Justice to account for his 'evasive' answers to the Senate Foreign Relations Committee in 1973, Helms pleaded *nolo contendere* to a charge that he had 'refused and failed to answer material questions' when he appeared before the Committee earlier. (*Nolo contendere* is a plea which does not admit guilt but subjects a defendant to punishment as though he had pleaded guilty.)

In November of 1977, after a long-delayed trial, Judge Barrington D. Parker found Helms guilty, suspended a jail sentence, but sentenced him to a year's probation and imposed a fine of $2,000. Judge Parker also lectured Helms on his behaviour. 'You considered yourself bound to protect the Agency whose affairs you had administered and to dishonour your solemn oath to tell the truth before the Committee. You now stand before the court in disgrace and shame.'

But Helms was not disgraced and shamed as far as his former CIA colleagues were concerned. A number of them held a private party for him after the brief trial, took up a collection to pay the fine, and warmly congratulated him on his staunch refusal to tell CIA secrets. Most Agency members felt that the Justice Department never should have brought the charges against him in the first place. Actually, they firmly believed, it had been the president of the United

States, Richard M. Nixon, who was the man responsible. But perhaps the Watergate affair had already visited enough disgrace on Richard Nixon.

Other baubles among the family jewels

The Helms disclosures were just a few of the baubles that were soon to be found among the CIA's precious and, until now, secret cache which came to be known in the Agency as the 'family jewels'.

On 22 December 1974, Seymour Hersh exposed another jewel to the light with a story in the *New York Times* that began: 'The CIA, directly violating its charter, conducted a massive illegal domestic intelligence operation during the Nixon Administration against and anti-war movement and other dissident groups in the United States, according to well-placed Government sources.'

Hersh's reference was, of course, to the ill-fated Operation Chaos. But now it appeared there was more to the operation than merely investigating dissidents to see if they had been motivated by communist agents. What hadn't come to light until now was the fact that for a considerable period of time there had been a secret operation that included opening private mail to see if the senders or recipients had any communist connections. This kind of censorship had been quietly conducted during World War II when virtually all mail between the United States and Europe had been secretly opened and read during a mail-processing layover in Bermuda, but to have such censorship carried on in peacetime shocked most Americans. Suddenly the CIA seemed to many people to have turned into a domestic Gestapo like that in Hitler's Germany.

(It should be remembered that the United States was never officially at war with North Vietnam, since there had never been an official declaration of war by Congress.)

Further investigation disclosed that the mail-opening operation had been going on for many years. It had begun, in fact, during the Eisenhower Administration in 1953. What it involved was secretly opening first-class letters to and from communist countries. Its purpose was to identify Soviet agents in the United States through communications with them from their communist bosses. But, and this was an important but, the mail-opening operation had continued right up to 1973, and any information that was obtained about anti-war activists who had connections with correspondents in communist countries was distributed among members of the intelligence community.

The Church Committee found that all such mail-opening activity was clearly illegal and turned its findings over to the US Justice Department. After a lengthy investigation the Justice Department announced that it would not prosecute anyone because 'the Department almost certainly would encounter the gravest difficulties in proving guilt beyond a reasonable doubt'.

Among the other valuable family jewels that Hersh unearthed was the fact that the CIA had 'maintained intelligence files on at least 10,000 American citizens'. Here again many Americans suspected that an American domestic Gestapo was at work, or that perhaps author George Orwell's predictions in his book *1984* were coming to pass and Big Brother was watching them.

But these files turned out to be not quite so ominous as at first appeared. What they were was the record of all American anti-war dissidents who travelled abroad and their connectons, if any, with foreign communist or communist-front organizations. This, of course, led directly back to Operation Chaos. What was now made public for the first time, however, was the fact that between 1969 and 1972 the CIA had hired as agents some twenty-five anti-war activists. These agents were supposed to travel abroad and identify communist-front groups to which American citizens were loyal. Unfortunately, several of these agents undertook their investigations within the United States to report on anti-war demonstrators and other dissidents. Since this was purely domestic activity it was outside the bounds of the CIA charter. All such activity was supposed to be conducted by the FBI. Here again was what the American public regarded as police-state activity by the CIA.

The Church Committee's report on assassination attempts

Among the most valuable of all the intelligence gems in the CIA's family jewels was all of the information about the rumoured assassination attempts by the Agency on foreign leaders. But in its report the Church Committee said that 'the CIA had not actually participated in the *successful* assassination of any foreign leader'. (Emphasis added.)

The Agency, the Church Committee report continued, had not planned the killing of Diem in Vietnam, General Schneider in Chile, or Trujillo in the Dominican Republic. But there was convincing evidence that CIA officials had planned the assassination of Lumumba in the Congo and Castro in Cuba, although none of these attempts had been carried out. In the case of Lumumba the Church Committee decided that there was evidence 'strong enough to permit a reasonable inference that the plot to assassinate Lumumba was authorized by President Eisenhower'. In the case of Castro the Church Committee ducked pinpointing the responsibility for the assassination attempts on the Cuban leader by saying, 'There was insufficient evidence from which the Committee could conclude that Presidents Eisenhower, Kennedy or Johnson, their close advisors, or a special group authorized such actions.'

In a final statement issued in the spring of 1976 the Church Committee stated flatly: 'Congress has failed to provide the necessary statutory guidelines to insure that intelligence agencies carry out their missions in accord with constitutional processes. Mechanisms for and the practice of congressional oversight have not been adequate ... The need to protect secrets must be balanced with the assurance that secrecy is not used as a means to hide the abuse of power or the failures and mistakes of policy. Means must be provided for lawful disclosure of unneeded or unlawful secrets.'

As a result of the Church Committee recommendations a permanent Select Committee on Intelligence was established by the Senate in 1976. A short time later a similar Oversight Committee was established in the House of Representatives. Earlier, Congress passed the Hughes-Ryan Amendment to the Foreign Assistance Act which provided that no funds could be spent by the CIA abroad for any covert action 'until the president finds that each such operation is important to the national security of the US and reports in a timely fashion, a description and scope of such operations to the appropriate committees of the Congress, including the Committee on Foreign Affairs of the US Senate and the Committee on Foreign Relations of the US House of Representatives'.

As a result of these several moves by Congress a president who is considering any covert action by the CIA must include in his considerations some 200 members of the Congress and their staffs. This has been widely heralded by many as the only realistic way that the CIA can be kept in check. Others have observed that it is impossible to preserve any kind of secrecy under such a system – and covert action or clandestine activity that is public knowledge loses its effectiveness.

The fact that the CIA's operations in Nicaragua and El Salvador in the mid-1980s were more or less public knowledge is just one of the end results of the new Congressional oversight legislation. There was a time when such CIA activity would have been truly covert. Today it is a matter for open public discussion.

This once again raises the question of whether or not there is a legitimate place for covert intelligence agency activities in a free society. It has been suggested that covert activity be removed from CIA jurisdiction and that the Agency simply be an intelligence-gathering organization as President Harry Truman apparently originally intended. Of further damage to CIA covert activities has been the vast amount of previously secret information that the CIA has had to divulge under the Freedom of Information Act. The Reagan Administration has endeavoured to stop the flow of CIA secrets by weakening the Freedom of Information Act, but it has had only limited success to date. As a result, members of the government trying to prevent even trivial information from leaking out have taken to classifying all of their papers 'Secret' and refusing to declassify them despite public requests to do so. This foolish situation of the classification of such things as intra-office memos and the like has yet to be resolved.

Those who defend the right of the CIA to carry on truly secret covert operations have suggested that what the United States needs is a law similar to that in Great Britain which is known as the Official Secrets Act. This makes the divulging of any classified information – such as the disclosures regarding the CIA's 'family jewels' – a criminal offence. But little headway has been made in getting a similar Act passed in the United States. CIA personnel sign an agreement never to publish anything about the Agency unless it is first cleared by the CIA, but America's free press would probably never stand still for forcing a Seymour Hersh to get his *New York Times* stories similarly cleared.

Interestingly, within recent months there has been a strong movement in Great Britain to repeal or at least modify its Official Secrets Act. This is because many members of the British legal profession believe that the Act is too sweeping in its scope. They feel it should be replaced by a legal code that would call for ciminal prosecutions only when national security is involved. As it is now the Official Secrets Act makes no distinction in the sentencing of offenders between minor infringements by civil servants and major violations of national security. Some critics even favour the adoption of legislation similar to the United States' Freedom of Information Act.

Those who oppose CIA covert activity insist that the kind of information about the Agency's clandestine role in Nicaragua, El Salvador and elsewhere in Latin America *should* have been exposed. Their reason for believing so is that such activities are actually part and parcel of United States foreign policy and should be guided by Congress and not just a president giving the CIA secret directions.

United States intervention in Latin America in general and Nicaragua in particular is certainly nothing new. After all, United States Marines were sent into Nicaragua in 1909, 1912, 1922, 1925, and were virtually stationed there between 1926 and 1933. The purpose of this intervention, however, was stated openly by the State Department: it was to protect US security and financial interests. Whether such military action in Nicaragua – and it has occurred elsewhere in Latin America – was right or wrong, popular or unpopular (it was most certainly unpopular with the Nicaraguans), it was nevertheless part and parcel of US foreign policy and openly acknowledged as such. Covert CIA activity in the mid-1980s is a form of conducting US foreign policy but a secret form in which Americans in their traditional free society feel they do not play a role.

Congressional action on Nicaragua

The US Congress made it clear that it no longer intended to act as a rubber stamp for further CIA action in Nicaragua and elsewhere in Latin America when early in 1985 it threatened to continue to withhold all funds for US-backed rebels or *contras* fighting the Sandinistas or current Nicaraguan government. Such funds had been cut off earlier, but the Reagan Administration had hoped to have them renewed by the new Congress.

The reason for continued Congressional disenchantment with the CIA was contained in a sixty-one page report issued by the Senate Intelligence Oversight Committee which continued to object to the secret mining of Nicaraguan harbours and the production of the guerrilla warfare manual that advocated assassination of Sandinista government officials. No adequate explanation of either of these activities had yet been given, the report pointed out. It remained doubtful that any adequate explanation would ever be forthcoming.

Nevertheless, the Reagan Administration continued to press for the release of at least $14 million to aid the rebels. Clearly, the CIA role in clandestine affairs, at least in Central America, remained in doubt if not in actual jeopardy.

10
The Soviet spy who came in from the cold

After a long period of receiving nothing but bad publicity the CIA was pleased to finally get some good press notices in the spring of 1978. This occurred when Arkady Shevchenko, a top Soviet diplomat at the United Nations and a former aide to the Soviet Union's Foreign Minister Andrei Gromyko, defected to the United States.

Because Shevchenko was the highest-ranking Soviet diplomat to defect to the West since the end of World War II, the news made world headlines. What was not immediately made known was something that was even more important to the United States. This was the fact that for two and a half years before he defected Shevchenko had been a highly successful agent for the CIA.

Although it was common gossip in intelligence circles after Shevchenko came in from the cold that he had been a CIA agent the fact was not acknowledged or made public until early in 1985 when his book, *Breaking with Moscow*, was published. The book was written with the aid of his American wife, Elaine, whom Shevchenko had married the same year he defected. It is probable that the CIA also had a hand in what the Shevchenkos wrote and what they left unwritten.

Naturally, neither the CIA nor Shevchenko was

eager to detail the kind of intelligence information Shevchenko had provided. But there could be no question that it had been valuable, probably the most valuable since Soviet general and intelligence officer Oleg Penkovskiy had provided both British Intelligence and the CIA with advance information about the building of the Berlin Wall to separate East and West Berlin and the size of the Soviet missile force at the time of the Cuban missile crisis during the Kennedy Administration. But Penkovskiy had never escaped. He had been caught and murdered by the KGB.

Many observers asked why the CIA had run the risk of having Shevchenko detected by the Soviets by using him as an agent for so long. The answer was twofold: first, it was the one sure way of learning whether he was not a double agent but indeed a genuine defector, and second, if he was genuine then the amount of valuable intelligence he could provide by remaining as a CIA agent-in-place was enormous. Quite obviously the risk proved worthwhile and Shevchenko's defection was not made public until the KGB had become suspicious of him. The question of why he was not assassinated by the KGB when his defection became known has not been answered. Shevchenko's diplomatic prominence may well have prevented the Soviets from taking such drastic action.

Background of a reluctant spy

Born in the Ukraine on 11 October 1930, Shevchenko was too young to fight in World War II. But he was old enough to experience the suffering along with his well-to-do merchant family at the hands of the invading

Germans. At an early age he became dedicated to the cause of world peace.

After the war Shevchenko was able to attend the better Soviet schools, including the Moscow State Institute of International Relations where the son of Foreign Minister Gromyko was also enrolled. It was through his friendship with young Anatoly Gromyko that Shevchenko got his start in the foreign service. He joined the Foreign Ministry in 1956 and advanced so rapidly that he soon was sitting in on meetings of the Politburo, the decision-making body of the Soviet Communist Party.

In 1960 Shevchenko was one of a small party of Soviet diplomats who accompanied Premier Nikita Khrushchev and Andrei Gromyko on an official visit to the United States where Khrushchev appeared before the United Nations. In 1963 Shevchenko became a regular member of the Soviet mission to the United Nations, serving on Gromyko's personal staff and eventually becoming Under Secretary for the UN, working with Secretary General Kurt Waldheim as a senior deputy. He served in this role until his defection.

Living with Shevchenko in New York were his Russian wife, Lina, whom he had married when he was twenty-one, and their daughter, Anna, who was eight years old when he first took up his UN duties. Their son, Gennady, who was in his twenties, was living and working as an engineer in Russia.

Lina Shevchenko was especially impressed with her privileges as the wife of a top-ranking Soviet diplomat. As a member of the *nomenklatura*, as this privileged Soviet class is called, she was able to buy all kinds of consumer goods that were far beyond her means or even available at home. In addition there was the privileged life at the Soviet recreational retreat at Glen Cove, Long Island, where Soviet diplomats and their families relaxed over long weekends (see *The KGB*).

For his part, Shevchenko was disillusioned by his privileged life as a diplomat. An idealist, Shevchenko could not accept the cynical way his colleagues totally ignored the principles on which the Soviet Union had been founded, principles that included a classless society. He was also disillusioned by the manner in which the Soviets used the United Nations as a great propaganda platform to promote the communist cause of world revolution and discredit the democratic efforts of the United States and other nations of the West.

Still vitally interested in the cause of world peace, all around him Shevchenko saw his colleagues ignoring that noble cause and spending most of their time feathering their own nests. This they did by buying automatic washing machines, dishwashers, cameras, television sets, video cassettes, stereo systems, records and tapes as well as crates of baby food, disposable nappies, dishes, flatware and clothing and having such booty shipped duty free back to the Soviet Union where such things were either unobtainable or prohibitively expensive. Some of these consumer goods the Russians kept for their own use when they returned home or sold on the black market. The Soviet personnel from clerks to top diplomats could afford to buy these consumer goods in the United States because their salaries – several times larger than they earned at home – were tax free, and their housing and medical insurance were provided at little or no cost.

Shevchenko did not spend all of his time at the United Nations. He was sent on several trips to Africa where he visited numerous poverty-stricken Third World countries. Here again he was disillusioned by the callous attitude of his Soviet superiors who sought to use these Third World people for political advantage with little thought about improving their economic conditions. Even Shevchenko's boss, Gromyko, whom Shevchenko greatly admired in most other respects, showed little genuine interest in or concern for the underprivileged. In fact, Gromyko's daughter, Emilia, once told Shevchenko, 'My father lives in the skies. For twenty-five years he has not set foot on the streets of Moscow. All he sees is the view from his car window.'

Eventually the thought of defecting to the United States was bound to occur to Shevchenko. Whether this idea was originally his own or was skillfully planted in his mind by a wily American agent is not known. Shevchenko insisted the idea was purely his own. Once the possibility occurred to him Shevchenko suggested it to his wife. But Lina was violently opposed to even discussing the subject. Consequently, Shevchenko reached the reluctant decision to act on his own.

US Ambassador Moynihan enters the picture

Daniel Patrick Moynihan who was then the American Ambassador to the United Nations later recalled that it was on Friday 5 December 1975, when an aide told him privately that Soviet diplomat Arkady Shevchenko had approached him about the possibility of defecting to the United States.

Moynihan at first refused to believe his aide. Were the Soviets setting some kind of trap?

But true or untrue the rumour would have to be investigated. Moynihan contacted both the CIA and the FBI.

For the next several weeks there was nothing but silence while the CIA worked quietly behind the scenes. Shevchenko was discreetly contacted by an agent in the UN library where a prospective meeting was arranged at a safe apartment in Manhattan. Shevchenko could arrive at the rendezvous or not, just as he chose. He chose to do so. The first step had been taken, a step along a path from which there was no turning back.

Shevchenko expected to be allowed to defect immediately and was obviously disappointed when he learned that this would not be possible. When he also learned that the CIA expected him, for a time at least, to become a spy he was further taken aback. He had no experience at espionage, he insisted. The CIA agent pointed out that on-the-job training was the best training of all. Fortunately, the defecting diplomat and the agent took an immediate liking to one another. They had a drink together to seal the bargain, and Shevchenko began his career as a spy.

Shevchenko's spy value

According to Patrick Moynihan, Shevchenko's greatest spy value lay in the fact 'that for the first time ever we had someone from deep inside the Soviet foreign policy system who could describe how it works'. This Shevchenko proceeded to do, but he also passed along some exceeingly valuable tactical or 'nuts and bolts' information about current and future Soviet plans. This was possible because he had ready access to all of his government's secret cable traffic at the United Nations.

One of the valuable facts Shevchenko revealed to the CIA was how the Soviet Union was cheating on arms-control treaties it had signed with the United States. Moscow had agreed in 1972 to destroy all of its weapons to be used in biological warfare. But at the time Shevchenko defected the Soviets were still producing such weapons. Needless to say, Shevchenko has been in favour of on-sight inspections within the Soviet Union as a clause in all future arms control agreements of any kind.

He also provided valuable information about how the Soviets were trying to encourage the pacifist movements in Europe, especially in West Germany, while discouraging the continued build-up of American military power on the Continent. He emphasized that world domination was still the Soviet goal and the only thing standing in the way of such domination was American military power.

One of the most controversial of Shevchenko's revelations was his belief that his mentor, Andrei Gromyko, as well as former Soviet Premiers Nikita Khrushchev and Leonid Brezhnev had serious ideas about treating the United States not only as an adversary or enemy but also as a partner in world affairs. Behind this startling proposition was the thought that perhaps together the two superpowers could reduce world tensions by some form of arms limitations and reduction.

State Department officials were extremely sceptical about Shevchenko's characterization of Gromyko, Krushchev, and Brezhnev as 'doves'. Gromyko especially had long been regarded as the most aggressive of Soviet 'hawks', and it was difficult to accept this sudden shift in attitude. Nevertheless, if it were true and if the Soviet military as well as the Politburo were also willing to listen to reason, then perhaps there was some cause for optimism about the Reagan Administration's renewal of arms reduction talks and even *detente* with the Soviet Union.

First hints of defection

Until 1977 Shevchenko regularly continued to visit the top secret Soviet cable room at the UN, quickly scanning the latest cables and committing their key contents to memory. Later he would meet his CIA and sometimes FBI contacts at the designated safe house or apartment. These meeting places were occasionally changed to avoid detection, and for many months that procedure was apparently successful. Then in the spring there was a sudden clampdown in Soviet security measures at the UN.

At a special meeting of the Soviet diplomatic personnel a KGB official announced that there had been attempts by the CIA to recruit members of the Soviet UN mission. All personnel were warned against such recruitment attempts and all contacts with foreigners would be regarded as suspicious.

That summer Shevchenko and his wife and daughter returned to Russia for a vacation. While on leave in a resort in the Caucasus Shevchenko was aware that he was being shadowed by the secret police. Back in New York, Shevchenko reported his anxiety to his CIA and FBI contacts who advised him to continue in his spy role for at least a few months but to be more than ever on the alert. Meanwhile, they would put in motion measures to protect him if he were suddenly arrested.

Early in 1978 Shevchenko received what he regarded as a final warning signal. He was requested to return to Moscow for 'consultations'. This was a technique with which Shevchenko through his KGB contacts was all to familiar. Once he returned to Moscow the game would be over. How suspicions about his activity had been aroused Shevchenko did not know, but he was certain a trap was being set for him.

Shevchenko used an excuse of a heavy workload to permit his being inside UN headquarters on a Sunday when the building was virtually deserted. There he called his CIA contact and arrangements were made for his final defection. His escape would mean deserting his wife and daughter, but as Shevchenko saw it there was no other way. Lina had steadfastly refused to listen to even a hint of their remaining in America, so he had never divulged any of his espionage work to her for fear of betrayal.

The escape plan went into effect several nights later. At their Manhattan apartment Shevchenko waited until midnight to make certain his wife and daughter were asleep. Then he crept out of the apartment and down a back stairway some twenty flights to the ground. He avoided using the front elevator for fear of encountering some other Soviet colleague who would be immediately suspicious about Shevchenko's leaving the building in the middle of the night carrying a suitcase.

Once on the ground outside the building he saw a white car parked in the street at the front of the apartment building just fifty yards away. But between him and the car there might be KGB killers lying in wait.

Shevchenko dashed to the waiting car. By the time

he reached it the rear door was open, and he leaped inside. In the front seat were two CIA agents. Immediately the car raced into the night towards a safe house in Pennsylvania.

Shevchenko's defection caused immediate turmoil among the Soviet UN delegates. His office was sealed and no visitors were allowed near it. His wife and daughter were quickly spirited out of the country and flown to Moscow. A few months later Shevchenko received the news that his wife Lina was dead. 'A suicide,' he was told. But Shevchenko knew she had been murdered. What happened to his daughter he did not know, but he was told she was still alive and safe and living with her grandmother in Moscow.

Slowly Shevchenko began to put his life back together. In December of 1978 he married Elaine, a court reporter whom he had met through his friend and lawyer, William Geimer. Soon he began to make a living through giving lectures and most recently from royalties following the publication of his book relating his defection from the Soviet Union. He is still a firm believer in and seeker for world peace.

Appendix: directors of the Central Intelligence Agency

The Central Intelligence Agency was officially established under the National Security Council by the National Security Act of 1947. It now functions under that statute, Executive Order 12333 of 4 December 1981, and other laws, regulations and directives. Before the CIA was officially established it operated semi-officially during 1946. Its directors have been as follows:

Rear Admiral Sidney W. Souers, 23 January 1946 – 10 June 1946.
Lt. General Hoyt Vandenberg, 10 June 1946 – 1 May 1947.
Rear Admiral Roscoe Hillenkoetter, 1 May 1947 – 7 October 1950.
General Walter Bedell Smith, 7 October 1950 – 9 February 1953.
Allen Welsh Dulles, 26 February 1953 – 29 November 1961.
John A. McCone, 29 November 1961 – 28 April 1965.
Vice Admiral William F. Raborn, Jr, 28 April 1965 – 30 June 1966.
Richard Helms, 30 June 1966 – 2 February 1973.
James Schlesinger, 2 February 1973 – 2 July 1973.
Wiliam Colby, 4 September 1973 – 30 January 1976.
George Bush, 30 January 1976 – 9 March 1977.
Admiral Stansfield Turner, 9 March 1977 – 23 January 1981.
William J. Casey, 23 January 1981 –

Bibliography

Bakeless, John, *Turncoats, Traitors, and Heroes*, J. B. Lippincott, Philadelphia 1959.

Bamford, James, *The Puzzle Palace*, Houghton Mifflin Co., Boston 1982.

Dulles, Allen, *The Craft of Intelligence*, Harper and Row, New York 1963.

Fremantle, Brian, *KGB*, Macdonald and Co., London and Sydney 1984 (paper).

Hood, Wiliam, *Mole*, W. W. Norton and Co., New York, London 1982.

Johnson, Haynes, *The Bay of Pigs*, W. W. Norton and Co., New York 1962.

Lawson, Don, *KGB*, Wanderer Books, Simon and Schuster, New York 1984 (paper).

Manchester, William, *The Glory and the Dream*, Bantam Books, Toronto, New York and London 1975 (paper).

Marchetti, Victor, and Marks, John D., *The CIA and the Cult of Intelligence*, Dell, New York 1980 (paper).

Meyer, Cord, *Facing Reality*, Harper and Row, New York 1980.

Powers, Thomas, *The Man who Kept the Secrets*, Alfred A. Knopf, New York 1979.

Rowan, Richard W., *The Story of the Secret Service*, Garden City, New York: Doubleday, 1937.

Shevchenko, Arkady N., *Breaking with Moscow*, Alfred A. Knopf, Inc., New York 1985.

Stockwell, John, *In Search of Enemies*, W. W. Norton and Co., New York, London 1978 (paper).

Willman, George (editor), *The Role of American Intelligence Organizations*, The H. W. Wilson Co., New York 1976 (paper).

Yardley, Herbert, *The American Black Chamber*, Bobbs-Merrill, Indianapolis 1931.

Index

Abel, Rudolph 54
Adams, Sue 92
Aguinaldo, Emilio 22
Albania 53
Alleged Assassination Plots Involving Foreign Leaders 9
Allende, Salvador 9, 97–100
American Revolutionary War, the 16–20
André, John 21
Arbenz, Jacobo 8, 50–1, 57
Arnold, Benedict 20–1
assassination, political 7, 70–7, 87–8, 97–101, 103–7
Atlantic Monthly (magazine) 73

Barnes, Tracy 60
Batista, Fulencia 57
Bay of Pigs, the 56–8
'Bender, Frank' 58
Bermuda 101
Bissell, Richard 49–60, 62, 64–5
'Black Chamber', the 30–3
Boland, Edward 7–8
Booth, John Wilkes 75

Brewster, Caleb 18
Breznev, Leonid 115
Brigada, La 58, 60, 62–5
Britain, Great 27, 35, 106
Bulgaria 34
Bureau of Military Information 24

Cambodia 42
Camp Peary 41, 45–6
Carranza, Nicolas 11
Carter, Jimmy 8
Casey, William J. 8, 11–12, 40
Castillo-Armas, Carlos 50–1
Castro, Fidel 9, 57–8, 60, 64–6, 70–4, 103–4
Chile 9, 97–100, 103
China 54
Christian Science Monitor (newspaper) 10–11
Chronicle of Current Events (journal) 38
Church Committee (1975) 9, 103–7
Church, Frank 9
Churchill, Malborough 27

Civil War, the 23–6
Clandestine Service *see* Deputy Directorate of Operations
codes and ciphers 27–32
Colby 90
'Cold War', the 15, 35, 79, 86
Colson, Charles 95
Congo, Belgian *see* Zaire
contras see Nicaragua
cryptonalysis 28; *see also* codes and ciphers
cryptography 28; *see also* codes and ciphers
Cuba 9, 22, 54, 56–66, 68–74, 76, 103
Cuban missile crisis 68–9
Culper Ring, the 16–21
Czechoslovakia 35
Czolgosz, Leon F. 75

DDI *see* Deputy Directorate of Information
DDO *see* Deputy Directorate of Operations
Davis, Jefferson 24
'Death Squads' 10–11
Deputy Directorate of Information 36–7
Deputy Directorate of Operations (Clandestine Service) 37, 49
Diem, Ngo Dinh 42, 86–8, 103
Diem, Nhu Dinh 87
Direccion Generale de Inteligencia (Cuba) 60, 74
Dominican Republic, the 9, 70–1, 103
Donovan, William ('Wild Bill') 15, 34–5
Dulles, Allen 27, 43–4, 50, 52, 56, 65; *The Craft of Intelligence*, 20
Dulles, John Foster 50

Eisenhower, Dwight D. 50, 54, 58–9, 61, 102, 104
El Salvador 10–11, 105–6
Ellsberg, Daniel 92–5

FBI *see* Federal Bureau of Investigation
'Farm, the' *see* Camp Peary
Federal Bureau of Investigation 72, 76, 84, 114, 116
Fielding, Dr Lewis J. 94–5
Fleming, Ian 72
Ford, Gerald 8, 74–6, 95
Fort Bragg 46
Fort Gulick 46
France 27, 35
Freedom of Information Act 105–6
Frente, the 58, 62
Fromme, Lynette 'Squeaky' 75
Frost, David 98
Funston, Frederick 22

'G–2' 26
Galazo, Oscar 75
Garfield, James A. 74–5
Geimer, William 118
Germany 15, 34, 101
Giancana, Sam 72
governments, overthrow of 7–9; *see also* assassination,

123

political
Grant, Ulysses S. 24
Green Berets, the 46, 89, 93
Gromyko, Anatoly 111
Gromyko, Andrei 109, 111, 113, 115
Gromyko, Emilia 113
Guatemala 9, 50–51, 57, 59–60
guerrillas 7, 88–9
Guevara, Ché 9
Guiteau, Charles J. 75

Haldeman, H. R. 95
Hale, Nathan 16
Hamilton, Alexander 18–19
Hawkins, Gains B. 92
Hawkins, Jack 60
Helms, Richard 60, 65, 84, 96–8, 100–101
Hersh, Seymour 98, 101–2, 106
Hinckley, John W., Jr. 75
Hitchcock, Ethan Allen 22
Honduras 10
Hoover, Herbert 31
Hoover, J. Edgar 84
Howe, William 16
'HUMINT' 33
Hungary 35
Hunt, E. Howard 94–5

Indian Wars, the 22–3
International Court of Justice 10
invisible ink 19–20; *see also* Sympathetic Stain
Iran 96
Italy 15, 34

Jackson, Andrew 74–5
Janos, Leo 73
Japan 15, 34
Jay, Sir James 19–20
Jay, John 19
Johnson, Lyndon B. 70, 73, 75, 80, 83, 86, 93, 104

KGB 38, 42, 45, 47, 110
Kennedy, Edward 10–11
Kennedy, John F. 49, 61, 64–6, 68–71, 73–7, 79–80, 86–8, 104
Kennedy, Robert 71
Korean War, the 62
Krushchev, Nikita 54, 69, 111, 115

Langley, Virginia 40–41, 44, 47, 82
Lansdale, Edward G. 72–3
Laos 42, 88–9, 93
Lawrence, Richard 75
Lincoln, Abraham 23, 25, 74–5
Livesey, Frederick 30
Lloyd, William A. 23–4
Lumumba, Patrice 9, 71, 103–4

MacArthur, Douglas 34
McCone, John 65
McCloy, John J. 76
McCord, James 95
McGovern, George 95
McKinley, William 74–5
McNamara, Robert S. 92
Manchester, William 63
Manson, Charles 75

124

Martinez, Eugenio 94–5
Meo people 88
Meyer, Cord, *Facing Reality* 99–100
Mexican War (1846) 22
Miami 58, 62
Military Information Division 26
Minh, Ho Chi 86
Mondale, Walter 8
Montagnard people 89
Moore, Sara Jane 75
Morse code 28; *see also* codes and ciphers
Moynihan, Patrick 113–4
Mulligan, Hercules 18

NRO *see* National Reconnaissance Office
NSA *see* National Student Association
National Detective Police 25
National Reconnaissance Office 56
National Security Agency (NSA) 32–3
National Student Association 78–9
New York 16–19, 21
New York Times (newspaper) 11, 93, 98, 101, 106
Nicaragua 7, 10, 12, 39, 51, 59, 62, 105–8
Nixon, Richard 83–4, 86, 93–6, 98–101
Nolan, Dennis E. 27
Norway 53

OSS *see* Office of Strategic Studies
Office of Naval Intelligence 26
Office of Strategic Studies 14–15, 27, 34, 38, 42, 60
Official Secrets Act 106
Operation Chaos 83–5, 101–2
Operation Mongoose 71–3, 94
Orwell, George *1984* 102
Oswald, Lee Harvey 73–7

Parker, Barrington D. 100
Pasternak, Boris, *Doctor Zhivago* 38
Peace Corps, the 44, 79–80
Penkovskiy, Oleg 110
Pentagon Papers, the 92–4
Philippines, the 22, 72
Phoenix Program, the 89–90
Pike, Otis 100
Pinkerton, Allen 23, 25
'Plumbers' Unit', the 94–6
Poland 34
Powers, Francis Gary 54, 67
Powers, Thomas 53–4, 88
Psychological Operations in Guerrilla Warfare 7, 12–13

Ramparts (magazine) 78–80
Rankin, James Lee 76
Ray, Manuel 62
Reagan, Ronald 8, 12, 74–5, 108, 116
recruitment 42–4
Richmond, Virginia 24
Roe, Austin 18
Roosevelt, Franklin D. 74–5
Roosevelt, Theodore 74–5

Rumania 34

sabotage 34
samizdat 37–8
San Ramon, Jose Perez 62
Sandinistas *see* Nicaragua
satellites 55
Schneider, René 9, 99, 103
Schrank, John 75
Sharpe, George H. 24
Shevchenko, Ann 111, 118
Shevchenko, Arkady 109–18;
  Breaking with Moscow 109
Shevchenko, Elaine 109, 118
Shevchenko, Gennady 111
Shevchenko, Lina 111, 113, 117–8
Shriver, R. Sargent 80
'SIGINT' 33
Sixty Minutes (TV programme) 91
Soviet Union *see* USSR
Spanish American War (1898) 22
Special Operations Executive (SOE) 34
Speakes, Larry 8
Stevenson, Adlai 64
Stimson, Henry L. 14, 31
Stockwell, John 39–40, 71, 89
Switzerland 27, 86
Sympathetic Stain 19–20
Szcule, Tad 70

Tallmadge, Benjamin 16–18
Thailand 88
Torresola, Griselio 75
Townsend, Robert 17–18, 21

training 44–8
Trujillo, Rafael 9, 70, 103
Truman, Harry S. 15, 33, 35–6, 74–5, 83, 105
Turkey 53

U–2 52–6
USSR 15, 34–5, 37–8, 45, 49, 52–6, 59, 69, 73, 76, 86, 109–18
United Nations 111–6, 118
universities 78–85

Van Deman, Ralph H. 27
van Lew, Elizabeth 24–5
Viaux, Romero 99
Vietnam 9, 42, 72, 103; *see also* Vietnam War
Vietnam War 40, 42, 46, 82–93, 102

Waldheim, Kurt 111
Warren Report, the 75–7
Washington, George 15–23
Washington Post (newspaper) 93
Watergate Affair, the 94–6
Westmoreland, William 91–2
Woodhull, Abraham 17–19
World War I 26–30
World War II 14–15, 26, 34–5, 49, 62, 101, 109–11

Yardley, Herbert Osborne 27–32

Zaire 71, 103
Zangara, Giuseppe 75